SOULFUL
BOBCATS

SOULFUL BOBCATS

Experiences of African American Students at
Ohio University, 1950–1960

Carl H. Walker

with Betty Hollow

Foreword by Roderick J. McDavis

Ohio University Press
1804 Books
ATHENS

Ohio University Press, Athens, Ohio 45701
ohioswallow.com
© 2013 by Ohio University Press

To obtain permission to quote, reprint, or otherwise reproduce or distribute
material from Ohio University Press publications, please contact our rights
and permissions department at (740) 593-1154 or (740) 593-4536 (fax).

Printed in the United States of America
Ohio University Press books are printed on acid-free paper ∞™

23 22 21 20 19 18 17 16 15 14 13   5 4 3 2 1

This book was made possible by grants from the Ohio University Office
for Diversity and Inclusion, University College, and the Office of the
Executive Vice President and Provost.

Unless otherwise credited, photographs appear courtesy of members of the
Soulful Bobcats.

Library of Congress Cataloging-in-Publication Data

Walker, Carl H.
  Soulful Bobcats : experiences of African American students at Ohio University,
1950–1960 / Carl H. Walker with Betty Hollow ; foreword by Roderick J. McDavis.
      pages cm
  Includes bibliographical references and index.
  ISBN 978-0-9667644-6-8 (pb : alk. paper) — ISBN 978-0-9667644-7-5 (electronic
: alk. paper)
  1. Ohio University—Students—History—20th century. 2. African American college students—Ohio—History—20th century. I. Hollow, Betty, [date]– II. Title.
  LD4191.O84W35 2013
  378.771'97—dc23
                                    2013027507

THIS BOOK IS dedicated to Dorothylou Sands and Howard Nolan, without whom neither our reunions nor this book would have been possible.

Dorothylou initiated the idea of a reunion for Ohio University's African American students who later became known as the "Soulful Bobcats." She was the glue that kept us together over the years by visiting, calling, and writing to share news of members of our group.

Though Dorothylou did not graduate from Ohio University, she helped create, develop, and maintain our university family, and her undying love for, and loyalty to, the university and us is in a class of its own. We have loved her over these many years and we thank her for all she has done for us.

Howard Nolan was also impressed with Dorothylou's idea and helped to give it life. As an alumnus, he had served on the university's Board of Trustees, Foundation Board of Trustees, and Russ College Board of Visitors; he had also received the Alumni Association's Medal of Merit. Consequently, he was able to put us in touch with the people who were key to the success of our reunions.

As a man who could make things happen, Howard was well respected by his Soulful Bobcat brothers and sisters. He was loved as well. When he died in 2011, many of the letters of condolence that poured in voiced the same sentiment: "He was truly one of us."

CONTENTS

ILLUSTRATIONS

Ohio University, Athens, and Race

18 Soulful Bobcats

Illustrations

x

1991 Reunion

Illustrations

FOREWORD

As THE FIRST African American and second alumnus to lead Ohio University, the understanding of what I represent as president of this great university is not lost on me, nor is the realization that I am where I am, in part, because of the path that was paved by other African Americans, including John Newton Templeton, Martha Jane Hunley Blackburn, and others.

Among these were the Soulful Bobcats, whose experiences as African American students at Ohio University during the 1950s set the stage for true integration. With each trial and hardship, these students laid the foundation for a culture of inclusion—a culture that defines Ohio University.

Because of the Soulful Bobcats and other African American student groups, today's African American experience at Ohio University is both unique and celebrated. Drawing on a rich legacy of diversity, African American students are now able to absorb OHIO's transformative learning experiences within a supportive, affirming, and positive environment.

Reflecting on my own Ohio University journey, I am among the many alumni whose OHIO experience has been enriched by the African American students who came before me. Thanks to their presence and success on campus, I had the same boundless dreams as any college student, regardless of race or ethnicity. Through my college fraternity, Omega Psi Phi, I was able to experience the spirit of camaraderie forged among the Soulful Bobcats more than a decade earlier.

Like all students during the 1960s, my college years were defined by the many social and political movements of the day—including, but not limited to, civil rights. Even so, my path to graduation was still very much tied to my predecessors—stretching all the way back to the 1828 graduation of John Newton Templeton, Ohio University's first African American graduate.

For me, as it is for so many Bobcats, history is very much alive and well on these bricks. But that reality comes with a responsibility to preserve our past.

Through the experiences of the Soulful Bobcats, this book captures a glimpse of Ohio University during the midcentury quest for racial equality. It is my hope that chronicling this important piece of African American history will ensure continued strength in diversity at Ohio University today and always.

Cordially,
Roderick J. McDavis
President

PREFACE

THE IDEA FOR this book was a result of efforts to organize reunions for a special group of African Americans* who were schoolmates at Ohio University during the 1950s. For several years, Dorothylou Sands had asked me to help with a reunion and, after retirement from my first career, I had time to give her request more attention. It seemed to me that a reunion sanctioned by the university would allow us to take advantage of the resources of the Alumni Association and to convene on the campus. In getting started, I called about five of our schoolmates and gave them assignments for the project. Howard Nolan contacted Dr. Alan Geiger, assistant to the president, who arranged a meeting for the two of us with President Charles Ping in April 1991. My wife, Frances Ramsey Walker, and I left Atlanta, Georgia, and joined Howard in Columbus, Ohio; then the three of us journeyed to Athens. Howard and I met with Dr. Geiger and later with President Ping, who was very gracious and understanding.

During that meeting, President Ping gave both Howard and me a copy of the 1954 book, *The History of Ohio University*, written by Thomas Nathanael Hoover. Professor Hoover's book contained little indication that Negroes had much presence at Ohio University. He did, however, include two sentences that said, "In these years [1824–35] at least one negro attended the university. The *Ohio State Journal* of September 25, 1828, reports that John Templeton, a negro, was a member of the graduating class of that year." Recently, I reviewed a two-volume work, *Black America: A State-by-State Historical Encyclopedia*, published in 2011, and it was no more generous in portraying the accomplishments of John Newton Templeton.

* Throughout the book, the racial designations (including plural forms) of "Negro," "Colored," "Black," and "African American" are used interchangeably to reflect the time periods being referenced.

Both books, in my opinion, understated the importance of Templeton's achievement in becoming, in 1828, Ohio University's first, and possibly the nation's fourth, African American graduate.

I also read *A Significant Presence: A Pictorial Glimpse of the Black Experience in Athens County, Ohio,* by Ada Woodson Adams and Nancy E. Aiken, which provided information about African American experiences at Ohio University and in the town of Athens. My pride in Ohio University was greatly enhanced upon reading the superlative book, *Ohio University, 1804–2004: The Spirit of a Singular Place,* by Betty Hollow. Her book was quite detailed in showing the full picture of Ohio University and its students and more than made up for the omissions of Hoover's 1954 history. I was particularly interested to see that it included memories sent in by former students, including a number of reminiscences by African Americans who were students in the 1960s and '70s.

With the help of the Ohio University administration and the Alumni Association, my schoolmates and I held the first "Soulful" reunion in August 1991. At the time, our average age would have been about fifty-four, and most of us had not seen each other for twenty-five or thirty years. However, we were eager to relive the joys of the close personal friendships that had been strengthened by our dependence on each other in the face of racial segregation—friendships that had not faded during all that time.

The name of "Soulful Bobcats" evolved from the name of our first reunion in 1991, which was advertised as a "Soulful Reunion." Later, "Bobcats"—the mascot of Ohio University—became a logical addition to our soulful designation. The success of that gathering was so overwhelming that it was followed by a second reunion in 2001 and a third in 2010. Before we convened for the third reunion, I asked the Soulful Bobcats to write their personal stories, with an emphasis on their experiences at Ohio University. We had realized during the intervals between reunions that, as time went on, we were losing more and more members of our special group, and a book could be important. We also realized the significance of our attending a white institution *before* the modern civil rights movement of the 1960s. Thus, the groundwork began for this book.

As my schoolmates began sending me their autobiographical sketches, I began to think about who we were in the 1950s in Athens, Ohio. At that time, racial prejudice and discrimination pervaded all aspects of American life. Members of our group, like other African Americans, lived with daily reminders that we were black; that did not change because we were in college. Most, if not all of us, had to trade the reality of racial prejudice for the challenge of meeting academic and personal goals. We were part of what has been called "the silent generation," but we wanted our voices heard— we were eager for change. Consequently, we dedicated ourselves to confronting the tasks before us in order to earn our degrees, the respect of others, and the rights due all American citizens.

Although our lives at Ohio University were fairly tranquil, we were not deaf to the stirrings and sounds of the civil rights movement that were put in motion following World War II. Imagine being a college student during that time! It was wonderful, and we had a collective feeling of optimism, especially after the Supreme Court decision in *Brown v. Board of Education* and the use of federal troops to enforce the decision. Such a stance by the national government was instrumental in shaping our hopeful outlook.

Our ambitions were fueled by dreams of success—dreams we inherited from our parents and elders. In the words of Soulful Bobcat Ejaye Johnson Tracey, "One thing that bonded the students of color was our awareness that not every high school graduate was offered the opportunity to attend college. . . . We were expected, by those who had sent us, to do well, keep out of trouble, and stay until we graduated with a Degree. By keeping our part of the bargain, we would be upholding not only our dreams, but also those of our families and ultimately our race."

This book of autobiographical sketches speaks of those dreams, of our collegiate experiences, and of our later accomplishments. It begins with an overview of race relations, attitudes, and mores, especially at Ohio University and in the town of Athens, before the Soulful Bobcats arrived and so describes the climate into which we moved when we chose Ohio University. These stories reflect the point in time between established segregation and the national movement towards integration as it played out in Athens and its university.

Carl H. Walker

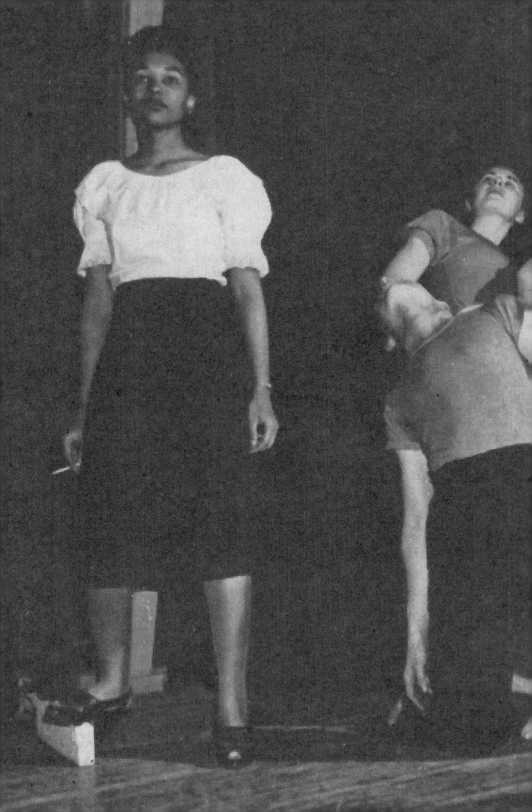

ACKNOWLEDGMENTS

MANY PEOPLE HAVE contributed to this book in both tangible and intangible ways, and I am grateful to all of them for their support, friendship, and cooperation.

First, no one has been more important than Tyrone Carr, Director of the Interlink Alliance and former special assistant to the president, who gave me excellent advice on today's Ohio University and arranged meetings for me with people who were essential to the project. Ty was first in line to assure me that this book could be done.

The support of President Roderick McDavis has been unsparing and inspirational. The ongoing support and assistance of Executive Vice President and Provost Pam Benoit and Associate Provost for Undergraduate Studies David Descutner have been essential. Thanks also to Arlene Greenfield and Brian Bridges for their encouraging advice.

I also acknowledge the help of university officials President Emeritus Charles Ping, Dr. Alan Geiger, former Provost James Bruning, Dr. Patricia Gyi, Patricia Cavender, Ralph Amos, Richard Polen, Connie Romine, and Cristie Gryszka, all of whom played key roles in bringing about the first reunion.

WOUB's Beth and Sam Venable were superb in recording interviews with some of the Soulful Bobcats. These have been transcribed and edited and are presented in the book as autobiographical sketches. Sam also provided a logo for the book cover that reflects the era and spirit of this alumni group.

Thanks also go to Soulful Bobcats Lois "Wicki" Green, Ada Woodson Adams, Jo Peters, Theodore Young, and Leon Ward who were willing volunteers for many tasks.

I am very grateful for Betty Hollow's enormous contributions to this book. Her information and insights allow us to present a book that chronicles the history of racial integration at Ohio University. Betty and I met at a fortuitous time and kept in touch, sharing ideas and work for almost three years. Using material from Ohio University's Mahn Center for Archives and Special Collections and from interviews with Athens residents, she wrote the introductory chapter. She also edited the autobiographical sketches.

Most of all, Frances Ramsey Walker deserves continuous applause for her patience and help in doing as much as she could in bringing the book to fruition during some of the most challenging times of her life.

And finally, my deepest appreciation to Gillian Berchowitz, the editor who refused to give up on this project that is so dear to the hearts of a few Ohio University alumni.

SOULFUL
BOBCATS

OHIO UNIVERSITY, ATHENS, & RACE

A Prelude to the 1950s

WHEN FRANK UNDERWOOD and Charles Wilson arrived at Ohio University in the fall of 1950, one of their first stops was at the office of Coach Carroll Widdoes. Both Frank and Charlie had earned varsity letters in several sports at their high school in Wintersville, Ohio, and, because of their outstanding abilities, Widdoes had recruited them to play football. Both had been awarded athletic scholarships, for which they were grateful, for it would have been financially difficult for either of them to pay for college without some financial assistance.

In most ways they were like the many other talented young men who earned their room and board by playing football, baseball, or basketball at the university. But in one singular way, they stood out. They were the first "colored" men to be actively recruited and offered athletic scholarships in the school's 146 years.

This change was significant enough to be talked about, and the talk made Underwood and Wilson realize that, by offering them scholarships, the university was making a commitment not only to them, but to minority

Manasseh Cutler Hall, completed in 1819, is the oldest college building in the former Northwest Territory. At the time of this photograph, the building had been covered with a white plaster façade. In 1948, an extensive renovation of Cutler Hall was completed, including the restoration of its original red brick exterior. 1925 *Athena. Courtesy of the Mahn Center.*

students who might follow them. What they didn't know then was what provoked the change. But years later, Underwood heard the story from the man who was responsible: John C. Baker, who had served as Ohio University's president from 1945 to 1961. According to Underwood, Baker said that one day in 1949, while he was watching a Bobcat ball game, he had a sudden realization. He said, "I didn't see any colored players, and I asked someone why we didn't have any colored players. They gave me some garbage, and I told them to get some!"

Though Baker's 1949 order to recruit African Americans created a stir, Ohio University's association with students of color was hardly new. In fact,

Arthur D. Carr, a member of the 1903 football team, was probably the university's first African American athlete. *Courtesy of the Mahn Center.*

the school was still in its infancy when John Newton Templeton, a freed slave, graduated in 1828. Edward J. Roye, who became the fifth president of Liberia, was on campus for a year in 1833. Joseph Carter Corbin, who later founded and served as the first principal of Branch Normal College of the Arkansas Industrial University, earned his BA in 1853 and MA in 1856. Sisters Minerva and Valerie Woodson, who were from the Athens area, attended in the 1870s.

Clearly, African American students had been allowed to attend the university, but during the school's first century only a handful had done so. And they had been more tolerated than welcomed. In the new century, their numbers began to increase. Between 1900 and 1920, the school had seventeen African American graduates. Among them was Arthur D. Carr, who donned an Ohio University sweater to play alongside the sixteen white members of the football team in 1903. He graduated in 1905 and went on

Ohio University, Athens, and Race

Above: The DuBois Club was founded in 1915 by Leonard Barnett, '16 (*inset*). 1916 *Athena. Courtesy of the Mahn Center.*

Left: Martha Jane Hunley Blackburn is now celebrated as the university's first female African American graduate. 1916 *Athena. Courtesy of the Mahn Center.*

Members of the newly reorganized fraternity, Alpha Phi Alpha. The chapter was established at Ohio University in 1919, but lost its charter due to insufficient membership. In 1956 it was reestablished. 1956 *Athena. Courtesy of the Mahn Center.*

to earn a medical degree at Howard University. Leonard Barnett graduated in 1916 after founding the Du Bois Club a year earlier. Other seniors pictured in the 1916 *Athena* were Frederick C. Seelig, Estella Clarissa Lee, and Martha Jane Hunley Blackburn; years later Blackburn was recognized as the school's first female African American graduate.

During 1919, at least ten African American men were enrolled—enough to establish a chapter of Alpha Phi Alpha, the first black Greek letter fraternity on campus. Then, rather dramatically, the numbers began to rise. Between 1920 and 1924, seventeen African Americans graduated. And perhaps this increase was just enough to concern the school's trustees and its new president, Elmer Burritt Bryan, who was inaugurated in 1921.

Bryan had a special interest in bringing more men to campus to balance the large number of young women who were attending the university's State Normal College. He proposed courses and activities with masculine appeal, such as engineering and athletics. In 1922, he encouraged the trustees to buy the old Masonic Hall to provide the men with some dorm rooms, a dining room, and space for their organizations. But it is reasonably safe to assume that he wasn't thinking of African American students—either male or female—when he made these proposals.

He made that clear in June 1922 when he agreed with the discriminatory action taken by the lessee of a student cafeteria in the university's Agricultural Building (now Tupper Hall). According to fourteen Negro summer school students who went there to eat on June 23 and 24, they were told they would be served only if they agreed to eat together (apart from white students) in a room in the rear. Humiliated and indignant, they informed others. Immediately thirty-six of the "Colored Students" at summer school signed a "memorial" of protest to Bryan and chose a committee to speak with him about such unjust treatment.

Bryan had said he "deplored the sensitiveness [of the situation] but on account of public opinion he felt that he was in accord with the segregation policy" of the lessee. When the students said they might have to take legal action, based on Ohio's 1884 Public Accommodations Law, the president told them that could "lead to reprisals" that would "prevent students from attending Ohio University" if they were barred from admission to their home state universities.

Though there is no evidence that the students took legal action—they were advised that such action would be expensive and ineffective—in 1923 Bryan and the Ohio University Board of Trustees agreed on the restrictive policy he had referred to when meeting with the students the previous year. In official language it said, "The University admits . . . graduates of the four-year high schools in Ohio . . . and all others (either in Ohio or in other states, provided their own state universities admit them)." This meant that no students could be admitted from states such as New York and New Jersey that did not have public universities, and that no African American students could be admitted from segregationist states such as Kentucky and West Virginia.

Although Bryan had told the trustees that too many colored students could have the effect of making Ohio University a less desirable place, he still hoped "to avoid criticism." Later, Professor Walter S. Gamertsfelder tried to cast the policy as an economic measure, approved to prevent the state of Ohio from subsidizing other states' students. But no one was fooled by this obviously racist policy, and some groups appealed to the governor to force the university to rescind it. However, no action was taken and the policy died quietly in the 1950s without ever being officially denounced or overturned.

A second policy with serious consequences for African Americans was approved after the university closed John Hancock High School in 1926. This model school, which had operated on the third floor of Ellis Hall since 1917, had been an ideal place for the university's secondary education majors to complete their practice teaching requirement. With its own high school no longer available, the administration planned to place its student teachers in Athens's city schools. After some negotiations, Athens school officials proposed a contract, and the university signed it—despite the fact that it banned all African American practice teachers. Again, some voiced outrage at the inconvenience and expense the exiled students would experience by being forced to finish their degree requirements in cities far from campus. Again, no action was taken to reverse the decision.

The city's insistence on this discriminatory policy is perhaps one of the best indications of racial attitudes that had existed in Athens for many years. During much of the nineteenth century, Athens had remained small and isolated, without much contact with outsiders, especially outsiders of color. According to Professor Robert L. Daniel, author of *Athens, Ohio: The Village Years*, before the Civil War only sixteen African Americans lived in Athens, and fifteen of them were free-born Ohioans. The 1870 census reported twenty-four African American households for a total of 140 people, and Daniel elaborates, saying that "a sizable proportion of the adults were

Hotel Berry, owned and operated by African American Edward Berry, was known for excellent food and service. *Courtesy of the Mahn Center.*

mulattos," who came to the village after the war, often from Virginia. Most were young people. Many were illiterate and so held menial jobs.

By 1890 blacks in Athens were developing a sense of community through membership in a number of organizations, including the African Methodist Episcopal Church, Mount Zion Baptist Church, and the local Odd Fellows Lodge. By the turn of the century, Frank Hall and James West had opened "eateries" for their own black community. Edward C. Berry, the black man who was called the "Horatio Alger of Athens," had become a well-known businessman. He owned

Edward Berry, the "Horatio Alger of Athens." *Courtesy of the Mahn Center.*

the elegant, very popular Hotel Berry on Court Street where he employed local blacks—but served only a white clientele.

Daniel makes clear that, in most ways, "without any public debate over the matter, Athens whites and blacks went their separate ways in social and religious matters." Most blacks lived in the "rowdy" West End alongside prostitutes and saloons. There were occasional "scuffles," but as long as "coloreds knew their places," there was little overt harassment. They were, to a large extent, "invisible." There was little to keep them in Athens, and by 1920 their numbers had declined.

According to Joanne Prisley, longtime Athens resident and former curator and acting director of the Athens County Historical Society and Museum, these were the attitudes that still prevailed in Athens when Frank Underwood and Charles Wilson arrived in 1950. But, in a broader context, these young men arrived during a period of transition, for Ohio University, for the residents of Athens, and for the country as a whole—a transition from institutional and de facto segregation to at least nominal integration. This transition, really a resurgence of earlier efforts to improve the status of Negroes in America, began, in part, as a result of World War II.

Effects of World War II on Civil Rights

Though the most dramatic decisions affecting race relations in America were made after the war ended in 1945, some events in the early 1940s were significant. During 1941, a wave of African Americans moved out of the South and into northern and western cities where defense industries were booming. They soon found that most new, well-paying, war-related jobs were reserved for whites. When President Franklin D. Roosevelt took no action to end the discrimination, A. Phillip Randolph, a labor organizer and president of the largely black Brotherhood of Sleeping Car Porters, threatened to lead a massive march on Washington. To prevent a possible riot, Roosevelt signed Executive Order 8802, prohibiting discrimination in defense industries and creating the Fair Employment Practices Committee (FEPC) to ensure the order's enforcement.

Following this victory, the National Association of Colored People (NAACP) promoted the *Pittsburgh Courier's* popular "Double V Campaign" for victory against fascism overseas and victory against racism at home; its legal efforts led to U.S. Supreme Court decisions that expanded African Americans' rights in voting, education, and interstate transportation. But it was military service, especially overseas service, that changed African Americans' own attitudes about their place in American society and led them to resist second-class citizenship.

Over a million African Americans served in the war and, though they were restricted to segregated units under white officers, they had the opportunity to show that they could be as disciplined as any other soldier. Only 125,000 served overseas and, until near the end of the war, combat was not an option. Then, the courage and skills of groups such as the Tuskegee Airmen of the 332nd Fighter Group, the Buffalo Soldiers of the 92nd Infantry Division, and the Black Panthers of the 761st Tank Battalion brought them a measure of respect, especially from the Europeans they encountered, who were much more accepting of African Americans than were whites back home.

When the U.S. government passed the GI Bill at the end of the war, many of these veterans seized the opportunity to enroll in colleges and universities across the country. Through education they hoped to change the future, for themselves and, possibly, for their country. And by the time the first of them graduated, issues of race raised by the war were making it harder for whites to defend segregation.

But even before the end of the 1940s, some individuals were taking steps towards integration. On August 28, 1945, Branch Rickey, general manager of the Brooklyn Dodgers, signed Jackie Robinson to a minor league baseball contract. Then on April 15, 1947, he promoted Robinson to the major leagues, making him the first African American to step on a previously all-white baseball field. On July 26, 1948, President Harry Truman signed Executive Order 9981, which stated that there would be "equality of treatment and opportunity for all persons in the armed services without regard to race, color, religion, or national origin." Neither Rickey nor Truman acted out of simple altruism: Rickey recognized that he could make money by fielding a black player; Truman was shrewd enough to grasp the political repercussions of African Americans' participation in the war. But both men firmly believed that racism was wrong.

Ohio University and Racial Issues: 1945 to 1950

For John C. Baker, who became Ohio University's new president in February 1945, the issue of race was not a top priority. The sheer number of veterans who were expected to enroll at the university over the next several years *was*. There were not enough classroom buildings and those that existed were dilapidated. Several important programs did not have national accreditation, and the faculty was underpaid and would soon be overworked. But Baker's most urgent concern was housing for hundreds, then thousands, of men—some with wives and children—whose arrival was imminent.

Baker quickly appointed a Coordinator of Veterans' Affairs and negotiated with government agencies for twenty-three temporary housing units and a large cafeteria building for the lower ground east of the campus, soon called "Hog Island" because every rain turned the bare ground into a sea of mud. Other temporary buildings were added to the College Green and to several off-campus sites. By 1946, the total number of students on

campus had increased from 2,030 to almost 5,000, and 75 percent of them were men. A house-to-house canvas of the town resulted in some 2,000 rooms, but that number was not enough to meet the demand, forcing some of the men to camp out in the men's gym, the local armory, the stadium, and in many nearby towns.

John Calhoun Baker served as the fourteenth president of Ohio University from 1945 to 1961. *Courtesy of the Mahn Center.*

"Hog Island," the lower ground east of the university campus, served as the location for veteran students' apartments. 1947 *Athena. Courtesy of the Mahn Center.*

For African American students, male and female, the problem of housing was not new. They had rarely been allowed in the limited dormitory space on campus and typically had to find their own accommodations, sometimes with local black families and often in rooming houses on the rough west side of town. Athens's white landlords remained staunchly conservative and were rarely willing to rent to them. As these students' numbers grew, the administration faced the fact that the university would have to provide some housing for them.

There is no way to tell how many of the veterans were African Americans, for the university no longer has records of veterans' admissions from that time. However, after the war the number of African Americans attending Ohio University went up and, not surprisingly, these students formed strong bonds. There is little official evidence that this was a concern to Baker, at least until June 1946, when a single sentence in the minutes of a board of trustees meeting reported: "He [Baker] discussed racial relations and organizations inclined to develop trouble in this connection."

There is, however, a less formal document, a long, undated memo from Baker, which must have been the impetus for his discussion of racial issues at the June trustees' meeting. The memo, titled "IS THIS THE BEGINNING OF RACIAL TROUBLE?" describes two events that were brought to Baker's attention within a relatively short time. First, "three Jewish girls and three colored boys had gone to the Berry Hotel," apparently to test the hotel's willingness to serve them. Though they were served, "the situation in the hotel dining room was very tense." In fact, it was so tense that it provoked a Mr. Proctor to call from the hotel to tell Baker that he was "very disturbed at the occurrence and didn't know what it meant."

The second event brought Baker to the offices of the *Post* at 11:00 PM one night to talk to a group of students representing veterans and various organizations, "the girl making the 'survey'" (of which Athens restaurants would serve Negroes), and the *Post* editor. The group showed Baker two photographs "of what seemed to have been the burning of a fiery cross" on the campus. Together, they speculated that the "whole thing might be a hoax" and agreed not to publicize it. However, the anonymous girl doing the survey had already reported the incident to three Columbus organizations, and the Urban League there had agreed to send representatives to Athens to "straighten out the matter with Westfall's," the Athens restaurant most adamantly opposed to serving Negroes.

In August a letter from sociology professor Arthur Katona informed Baker of a similar survey that had been conducted in 1944 by members of the Campus Religious Council as part of an agreement with "student leaders" to call off a threatened "mass demonstration." Katona cautioned the president that racial incidents such as this earlier one and the spring's alleged cross burning could cause great harm to the university and the community and advised him to "thrash out" the matter with "a friendly get-together of university administrators, town business men, and law enforcement officials." According to Baker's handwritten comment on the letter, he took this advice and "talked to business men."

The only other obvious information about efforts to integrate Athens restaurants comes from minutes of Los Amigos, a club founded by Lawrence A. Gibbs in February 1947. Its organizers wrote bylaws in April, applied for status as a campus organization in September, and held a general meeting in the art gallery of Chubb Library on October 16, 1947. Thirty-seven men and women attended and thirty-three signed on as the club's founding members. They elected Waldon Torrence, president; Bettye Dobson, secretary; Nelson Peck, vice president; Monica Rowe, treasurer; and Araminta Young, social chair. They also approved a constitution with the following preamble:

> We the Negro students of Ohio University do hereby establish Los Amigos to provide social and spiritual activities, cultural and intellectual advancement for its membership and for any person, regardless of race, color or creed, so desiring to enter the ranks of this organization.

Providing social activities was initially the first priority of the group for, although a few members were joining other campus organizations, they were excluded from the unending round of dances, parties, and events that constituted student life. But at the December meeting, A. Bernard Smith reported that an "interfaith group" was planning an inclusive club, and by the spring of 1948 issues of race and reports of the "interfaith group's" activities were brought up with increasing frequency at Los Amigos meetings. In March, DeLouis Broughton said, "We should stress social integration on campus and in the community." A month later, the club's minutes report that "Mr. Thomas spoke of the racial issue present here, now. He feels that this group should definitely take a stand."

YOU'LL FIND YOUR FRIENDS AT "B-MORE'S"

Quick and Friendly Service

BLACKMORE'S

Blackmore's was one of the Athens restaurants opposed to serving African American students. 1948 *Athena. Courtesy of the Mahn Center.*

In April 1948 Rowe reported that an "Interfaith Committee" had started a petition to integrate all Athens restaurants. The forms were available at the Mount Zion Baptist Church and could be circulated by anyone, although it was suggested that they be "reworded for the townspeople." She added that Dr. Edward Taylor, faculty advisor to Los Amigos, was "quite happy" that students might petition on a racial issue involving local residents.

Results of the petition drive were reported on May 1. Many townspeople had objected to the "movement," but some 2,333 people—most of them students—had signed. Places that served all comers were Quick's, White Crest, the Diner, Glenn's, and Carl's. Those that refused service to Negro students were the Berry, Esquire, Blackmore's, and Westfall's. According to the owners, their objections were "economic."

In some ways, members of the campus community were just as insensitive as those local businessmen. For example, the editors of the 1948

The 1948 *Athena* presented pictures of a minstrel show organized and performed by sorority pledges. 1948 *Athena. Courtesy of the Mahn Center.*

Members of Los Amigos, organized in 1947 as a social club open to all Ohio University students. 1948 *Athena. Courtesy of the Mahn Center.*

Athena gave a full page to Prep Follies, an annual performance presented by sorority pledges. According to the text, "A Dixieland chorus, end-men, and skits by each sorority featuring songs such as 'Mammy', 'Carolina in the Morning', 'Summertime', and 'Hello, My Baby', brought back the spirit of the old-time minstrel show to the stage at Memorial (Auditorium)." In four photographs, the sorority pledges, in blackface with exaggerated smiles, sing and dance on the deck of the steamboat *Robert E. Lee.*

Somewhat ironically, in the same edition of the *Athena,* the editors also gave a full page to the new campus organization, Los Amigos. A formal photograph presents twenty-five of the group's forty members; an informal shot shows club secretary Bettye Dobson leading an interracial group in Christmas caroling. The text announces the club's purpose: bringing "social activities to the Negro students on the campus."

Bettye Dobson leads caroling at a Los Amigos Christmas party open to the campus. 1948 *Athena. Courtesy of the Mahn Center.*

This yearbook also included more informal "snaps" of Negro students than previous yearbooks had. Among those included were Bob McCoy, as a member of the Wesley Foundation; Charles Stewart, as the photo editor of the *Athena*; and "honey-voiced" Bettye Dobson as a singer in "OU Kids." That fall Los Amigos was invited to participate in the activities of the Campus Affairs Committee, the "official executive committee of extracurricular life." The organization also agreed to work with the Religious Action League "on prejudice in the city"; together these two groups concluded that legal action would be necessary.

In January 1949, Broughton reported on the progress of their investigation, saying, "this year's action has been rather fast. Four testing groups have been set up . . . Twelve restaurants will be tested. Two Negroes, two Jewish, two Christians compose the testing groups." The first tests would

Above: Bob McCoy (*front row, far right*) with other members of the Wesley Foundation, "a national movement for students of Methodist preference." 1948 *Athena. Courtesy of the Mahn Center.*

Right: Chuck Stewart was the first African American photography editor of an *Athena* yearbook. 1948 *Athena. Courtesy of the Mahn Center.*

Bettye Dobson, singing in "OU Kids." 1948 *Athena. Courtesy of the Mahn Center.*

be at the Buckeye, Blackmore's, and Westfall's. Broughton again stressed that there would be court action and said, "It is definite that the university will not assist in this—plan." By April, Blackmore's, the Rainbow, and the Buckeye had agreed to serve Negroes on two conditions: *Do not congregate in one restaurant*; and *No rowdiness.*

Though there were still a few holdouts among restaurant owners, definite progress had been made on that front. Consequently, Los Amigos members turned their attention to discrimination in other areas. In May, Peck reported, saying, "there is no interraciality in the dorms." He proposed that the university stop requiring prospective students to state their race, creed, and color on their admissions applications.

Though members of Los Amigos continued to feel that they were not sufficiently integrated into the social life of the university, they were making their presence known, both socially and politically. Increasingly, African American students were included in honorary fraternities; some members accepted the Wesley Foundation's invitation to join its choir; others began to participate in intramurals. The group worked with the YMCA, YWCA, International Club, and others to organize a new club, the Melting Pot, to "bring unity" to campus. They approved of the Progressive Club's lawsuit against Westfall's restaurant and supported the club in arranging a mass meeting of students, faculty, and Athens residents to give them a "better understanding of the Negro problem in Athens." President Baker received a letter from the Progressive Club informing him, personally, of the lawsuit and the planned mass meeting. He was encouraged to attend, along with members of his administration.

As the decade ended, Ohio University's Negro students could feel that they had done their part in the transition to broader civil rights both on and off the campus. They had challenged Baker and his administration to end discrimination at the university and in Athens; they had worked with other groups to integrate Athens restaurants; they had created a club to provide social activities for themselves and other interested students; they had endured a variety of humiliations, large and small; and, through it all, they had avoided outright confrontation and violence. They would be followed in the next decade, the 1950s, by a cadre of students with similar goals and attitudes. Eventually some of this latter group would reunite and call themselves the Soulful Bobcats, all of whom now express gratitude for their experiences at Ohio University.

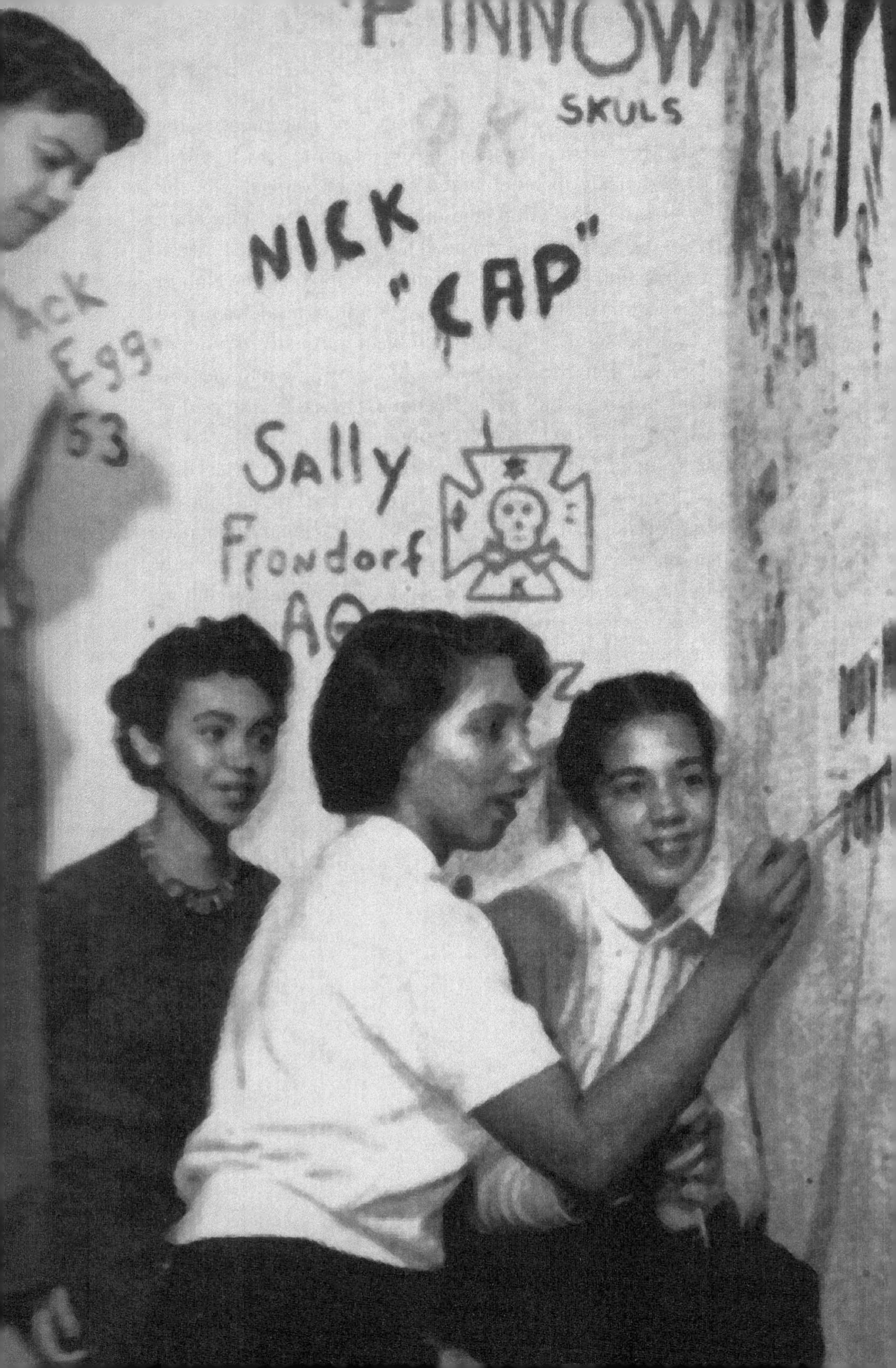
SKULS
NICK
"CAP"
Egg
53
Sally
Frondorf

18

SOULFUL BOBCATS

Autobiographical Sketches

WHO WERE THE students who became the Soulful Bobcats? Where were they from? What influenced them to seek university degrees at a time when fewer than 20 percent of American high school graduates were college bound? What academic, social, or racial problems did they encounter on the campus and in Athens? What were their successes? Who and what have they become?

Of the eighteen former students who submitted autobiographical sketches for this book, fourteen graduated from high schools in Ohio. Two spent their early years in Alabama, one was from Pennsylvania, and another was a West Virginian. Whether they came from near or far, all came from families that believed education was important, if not crucial, to their personal growth and success in a culture where prejudice and discrimination were the norm. Some were encouraged by counselors, teachers, or coaches to win scholarships or other financial aid that could reduce college expenses. With hard work, most were able to meet the challenges of the classroom, including the attitudes of some unsympathetic or openly discriminatory professors. And there was both prejudice and discrimination. Most irritating on a daily basis were the difficulty associated with hair care and the lack of social life beyond what they could create for themselves. Most humiliating were instances in which they were refused service in public places. Most frightening were a few occasions when violence seemed inevitable.

These challenges resulted in the students' local civil rights efforts. They pushed for a barber who would cut the men's hair, they tried to integrate the uptown bars, and they established two black fraternities and a black sorority. When solace was needed, they turned, most often, to each other, creating a home away from home, a community within the larger university community. A few were fortunate to have professors who became mentors, even friends. Virtually all of them participated in extracurricular activities whenever and wherever they could, playing sports, singing in choirs, dancing at the Bunch of Grapes Room in the student center, playing card games, and winning recognition for athletic and academic success. Many had jobs, operating the switchboards in dorms or serving in cafeterias. They chose majors in education, speech therapy, business, photography, journalism, or engineering—majors that would allow them to find jobs and serve in their communities or that would fulfill lifelong dreams. All but two of the men served in the military, either as volunteers or draftees. With support from their families and through their own determination and courage, they left Ohio University to lead rich, successful lives.

The Decade's Earliest Arrivals

Between 1950 and 1953, before the Supreme Court ruling in *Brown v. Board of Education* declared segregation in education unconstitutional, the first group of students who now call themselves the Soulful Bobcats enrolled at Ohio University. The first four—J. Beryl Hannon Dade, Frank Underwood, Lester N. Carney, and Lemuel "Rip" Nixon—were athletes, one of whom became an Olympic medal winner.

The first two, J. Beryl Hannon Dade and Frank Underwood, came in the fall of 1950. Though they didn't know each other when they arrived, it didn't take them long to meet and discover that they had things in common. Both came from predominantly white schools in Ohio. J. Beryl, as

The student center was one of the few places in town where African Americans could dance. 1955 *Athena. Courtesy of the Mahn Center.*

she was known then, had been one of only two Negro students in her graduating class at Shaker Heights High School. Frank, who graduated from Wintersville High School, had also been one of only two Negro students in his class; as a senior he had been elected its president. As a result, neither was intimidated or challenged by being part of a very small minority on the essentially white college campus in Athens.

J. Beryl Hannon Dade, 1950–54

J. Beryl and Frank had enjoyed a variety of sports in high school and had gained confidence from their successes on playing fields. J. Beryl was encouraged by her parents to be a participant rather than a spectator and so had been an enthusiastic member of her high school volleyball, baseball, basketball, and field hockey teams. She was also involved in Girls' Gym Leaders, Y-Teens, Red Cross, Honor Study Hall, and the choir. She continued her involvement at Ohio University, which she had chosen with the advice of a wonderfully understanding guidance counselor. However, on her first day on campus she encountered a situation that could have turned her against the place. Instead, she took it in stride.

Upon arriving at Ohio University and going through the first day, I reached my dorm room. The young lady in the room was in the process of taking her possessions to the next room. She said that she had settled into the wrong room and should be in the next room. To this day "Mir" (Miriam Boyd) and I have remained friends. During our days at Ohio University, and also after graduation, we visited each other's homes. Mir is white and I am black, though on paper one would not be able to tell the difference between us. My high school was about forty-five minutes from Mir's hometown, and it had a similar racial makeup as Mir's. The third roommate was Mary Raby, from Washington DC, who had an outstanding reputation.

    Over the years it was discussed that the room change/mix-up was a matter of no whites rooming with blacks. That was then. Though that was not a stated policy, it was a policy in practice. This happened in 1950, but by June 1954 requests were being taken. Whether granted at that time I do not know.

In spite of this incident, J. Beryl considered Lindley Hall her home.

Lindley Hall, our dorm, was large and, though we were a diverse population, we were a family. That was the atmosphere at Ohio University. Your dorm was your home and family. At the end of the first semester all residents on the south side of Lindley were moved to other areas of the building. That was the beginning of the south wing addition. My roommate, Mary Raby, and I both applied for the position of floor representative to the dorm council. We both received assignments. My location was the second floor of the south wing. For the next three years my roommate was Shirley Redding. On the corridor we were a real family, sharing, caring, and knowing about each other. Serving on the dorm council was one of the activities of my living in Lindley. I was not too welcomed at dorm lock-up time, but that too passed. Being the switchboard operator created a familiarity on both sides of the phone. My dorm friends and their phone contacts always made for campus familiarity.

Though J. Beryl does not mention it in her biography, she, Underwood, and Wilson became members of Los Amigos. However, by 1952 the group's membership had declined, perhaps because it had served its purpose; virtually all Athens restaurants were integrated and Alpha Phi Alpha fraternity would soon take up the slack in providing some social life for African American students. The one political activity that J. Beryl does report in her biography had to do with hair care, which was an issue for virtually all students of color on the campus. For the women, it was finding the privacy to straighten their hair with hot combs in their dorm rooms; for the men, it was getting haircuts. On one occasion, the black male students recruited J. Beryl to test a local barbershop.

A pre–civil rights event that was organized by the black male students had to do with male haircuts and the local barbershop. I was asked by the group to go to the barbershop to get a haircut. My dear friend, Mir, went with me. I got the haircut and left. I don't know the follow-up, but a black head of hair was cut.

Among J. Beryl's many other activities, sports came first.

In the area of sports, my life at Ohio University mirrored my high school years. The Lindley swim team was strong in the annual TKE [Tau Kappa Epsilon] competition. For three years the underwater swim team was number one. It was an accepted fact that Lindley would take first place. For those three years the same two swimmers were paired. I was the kicker in that pairing.

The Women's Athletic Association was invigorating and totally involving. Skills and friendships were always being developed. In the fall of 1953, my senior year, Ohio University hosted the Mid-American field hockey games. The Mid-American team was selected. I had the good fortune to be chosen for a wing position on the team to play in Bloomington. To make sure that nothing prevented my getting on the bus for the trip, my floor family and dorm friends made sure I followed everything as required. Participating in the sports that were offered over the four-year period—1950 to 1954—gave me a "Flying O" and, by the end of spring 1954, a "Varsity O."

The Canterbury Club [at the Episcopal Church of the Good Shepherd on campus] was another close affiliation. Learning, sharing, understanding, and community connections were the unifying focus of the group. There were meals, religious retreats, dances, and involvement with town members.

As a black student, education and learning all and everything presented was the priority and goal/aim in order to achieve whatever you desired. This belief was from the early years through college. The College of Education was a road well chosen. All experiences and activities laid a pattern to be followed in the years ahead. While my children were in college, I was teaching and returned, on a part-time basis, to switchboard work at the same time.

Frank Underwood, 1950–54

Sports gave Frank the entrée he needed to become a college student. He was a wide receiver on his very successful high school football team, and he played two or three other sports as well. By the time he graduated, he had earned a record nine varsity letters. In an interview years later, he described his early years.

It was my credo in high school and in college to just strive to do the best that I could do—to just be the best that I could be. I think that—to this day— I subscribe to that idea. For instance in high school my academic record wasn't that strong, but my social record was pretty good. I was a leader of my classmates. I was president of my senior class [which had only two Negro students]. I believe I was respected by most of my classmates. I was an achiever in their eyesight.

I was participating in so many sports because I wanted to find out which sport would get me a scholarship to college. I really wanted to go to college, and I knew my family couldn't afford to send me. I thought that if I was a good

Frank Underwood (number 81) was one of the first two African Americans to be offered athletic scholarships at Ohio University. 1952 *Athena. Courtesy of the Mahn Center.*

enough athlete, I would be able to get a scholarship. Football was it. Football gave me the opportunity to go to many colleges. I chose Ohio University. Don't ask me why I chose OU, but I did ... and I'm happy for my choice to this day.

Incidentally, my coming to Ohio University, along with a good buddy of mine who is now deceased, Charlie Wilson, meant that we were the first two black athletes to get athletic scholarships to Ohio University. It was talked about within athletic circles, and possibly on campus too. It was revolutionary. It was change. The university was endorsing black athletes by providing scholarships. The university had never done that before.

Coach Carroll Widdoes with Ted Jackson. 1954
Athena. Courtesy of the Mahn Center.

Ted Jackson (*left*)
and Charlie
Wilson (*below*)
were members
of the 1953
championship
football team.
1953 *Athena.
Courtesy of the
Mahn Center.*

I recall that
he [Coach Widdoes] called Charlie Wilson and
me into his office when we first arrived on
campus. He commented to us that he wanted to
make sure we were as pleased as he was that we
could be here. He stated that there would be
some opposition to our being at OU. He told us
that, and he assured us that he didn't think the opposition would be great, but
that he was four-score behind us. He was the messenger, I guess, who affirmed
why we were here.... He did his best to implement the boss's [President John
Baker's] desires.

I knew that what was happening was historic. The barriers were being
broken, and I knew that what was happening would open the door for
more minorities.

Though Frank and Charlie were somewhat prepared for being very
much in the minority in college (as they had been in high school), things
weren't necessarily easy.

In his interview, Frank recalled a time when he was traveling out of
town with the football team.

Soulful Bobcats

One incident comes to mind. That was about traveling. We traveled on the team bus. In Huntington, West Virginia, we played Marshall. There were two of us [African American players]. It was our freshman year. There was Charlie Wilson and me. We could not stay with our teammates. We had to stay somewhere else. That resonated strongly with me, of course. As far as other teams being integrated, I never had any challenge from the opposing players.

He also described the lack of social life for Negro students on campus— and the ever-present problem of hair care.

Well, there were no African Americans on the staff or on the faculty of this university. The only people of color you would see would be working in the dormitories or in the cafeterias. It wasn't that bad. I know I have heard some of my friends, who were from the inner city, assert that it was kind of a culture shock.

It wasn't a shock for me. I acknowledge the facts. We hardly had any social activity off campus. It wasn't as if somebody said, "No, you can't be here or come here. No blacks allowed, et cetera." That wasn't necessarily the case. You just knew that you weren't welcome in certain places. The barbershops would not cut our hair. We had to get our hair cut in The Plains. When we needed haircuts, the black barber here in Athens wouldn't cut our hair either. It was probably because of his business. If his other customers would see us sitting there, maybe they would no longer come to him. Maybe he was afraid that they would go down the street or to somewhere else. Those kinds of things existed. As far as the campus, I never had any negative experiences on campus. In fact, my experiences were positive.

For whatever reason, [Baker] chose me as a conduit to find out what was going on with the African American students. So periodically, I would get little notes in my box over at Scott Quad saying that Dr. Baker wanted to see me at a certain time. We would just sit down and talk about how things were going. I appreciated and respected him so much for his sensitivity to what was or was not going on. I liked his trying to find out the reality of it all. We did talk periodically. I guess he would wake up in the morning and think, "I wonder how the black students are doing?" He was a good man. He truly was. I really appreciate him.

In 1953, Ohio University's football team won the Mid-American Championship (MAC) for the first time. Frank says, "I like to think that Les and I had something to do with that."

Lester Nelson Carney, 1952–53 and 1957–59

The "Les" Frank Underwood referred to was Lester Nelson Carney, another gifted athlete who came to Ohio University and joined the football squad in 1952. Like Underwood, he was a graduate of Wintersville High School, where he had run track, played football, baseball, and basketball, and earned nine varsity letters. His unusual story follows.

We were probably one of the few [high] schools where you could play baseball and run track at the same time, because we only had two coaches. Each of them coached two sports. The football coach stressed that if you didn't run track, you couldn't play football. During the three years we [he and Underwood] played together—two years on varsity—we only lost one game. That was during Frank's senior year. During my junior and senior years, we went undefeated.

Like Underwood, Les would not have been able to attend college without a scholarship. His great success during his last two years of high school ensured that he was recruited to play football at several colleges, including Florida A&M and Ohio University. He chose the Ohio school in spite of having to pay for his own bus ticket when he was invited to campus in the spring of 1952—something, he says, that would never happen today. His first days on campus were a bit unorthodox as well.

Finally in the fall of 1952, I arrived on campus and moved into "the barracks" on the East Green. As my parents, my brother, and sisters were leaving, my dad walked over, gave me a hug and pressed two dollars into my hands, kissed me on the cheek and said, "Son, that's all I have and good luck." When they left, I shed a couple of tears, put on a V-neck sweater, and walked uptown to see a movie. I thought that I was now a full-fledged college student. Little did I know, but I found out on Monday morning when I tried to register for classes, that I was not even enrolled. I had only completed the football scholarship papers, so I had to start from scratch and go through the entire enrollment process, taking many tests, getting shots, and everything else. At the end of the day, I was finally an Ohio University student, but I still had to attend freshman football practice later that day.

After a month or so I had my first encounter with something that was totally different and unexpected to me. When I wanted to go get a haircut, I was told by some other colored students that in order to get our hair cut, we had to go to Mr. Thompson's house out in The Plains. I later found out that President Baker had set up those arrangements prior to more "coloreds" enrolling in school. There was the colored barber in town working in a "white" barbershop, but he probably would have lost business had he cut our hair.

We even got "funny looks" when we went into some of the uptown restaurants to get something to eat or were just walking around. But all in all, things (race-wise) pretty much took care of themselves, and there were not very many problems, in, on, or around campus. We did get to see many more "coloreds" (the townies) when we went to Mount Zion Baptist Church on Sundays and other days to have social gatherings. Sometimes good things happen because of bad circumstances. By having to go to Mr. Thompson's for our haircuts, I happened to see and meet his lovely little daughter [Lois Thompson Green, OU '60]. I'm still happy to have her as a "dear and loving friend."

As Les says, having to go out of town to get his hair cut was unexpected and annoying, but he made the best of the situation and built a valuable friendship. Unlike Underwood, who had come to the university two years earlier, he did not experience any racial problems when he traveled with the football team. If they stayed overnight, he slept in the same hotel as his teammates. However, it was a potential travel problem involving another Ohio University team that led Les to run track and eventually become an Olympic medalist.

Les Carney, '59, Ohio University's first track All-American, won all but one of his college races. In 1960 he competed in the Rome Olympics, where he won a silver medal. *Courtesy of Ohio University Athletics.*

After a very successful freshman football season and competing well in the spring football practice, I tried my hand at baseball. When I was in high school I had played pretty good baseball, and for two years during that time I worked out with the Philadelphia Phillies. I was halfway decent. When I came to Ohio University, they had the best baseball team in the mix. I went out for the team as a freshman. I played and scrimmaged. I thought I was competing strongly, but after a week or so of practice, the coach came to me and suggested that I try out for the track team.

At the time, I had no idea why the suggestion was made. Much later, I learned that the baseball team made a yearly "Southern baseball practice trip," and "Coloreds and Whites" weren't allowed to stay in the same hotels or even eat together. What a strange way of hearing something from the coach that later would turn out to be one of my blessings in disguise. As it turned out, running track for Ohio University, I lost one race as a freshman and then never lost another.

My sophomore year started as mundane as could be. I made the varsity football team (second- or third-team running back), had good success in school, and had many new friends. To help in meeting the many new friends we would sit on the wall facing Lindley Hall [a female dorm on South Court Street] and ogle the freshman girls checking into the dorm. Since I was now an upperclassman, I would invite some of the "freshies" to have a coke, meet and study at the library, hang out in the student center, or go to the campus movies. I could be a big-time spender for a dollar or two.

Bessie Owens Grant and Les Carney relax in a cafeteria booth.

Going out with your favorite girl had its good endings because all of the girls had "hours" and had to be in their dorms by 10:00 PM on weekdays and midnight on weekends. The best part was when they turned out the lights around the central desk about ten or fifteen minutes prior to the dreaded "hour." Since it was always a crowded and packed area, you heard a lot of "hissing, sighing, moaning, and smacking" and saw a lot of smeared lipstick, messy hairdos, and red faces when the lights came back on. Everyone made hurried exits, the boys outside and the girls upstairs, as the house mother stood guard. I can only imagine some of the conversations afterwards.

The 1953 football team was very successful, becoming the first Ohio University football team to win the Mid-American Football Championship. I'm happy to say I had a hand in that. After a few games I was promoted to first team (the only sophomore on that team) and ended up making MAC honorable mention. Other than that, the highlights of that season were taking my first-ever plane trip to a game at Harvard, having my dad see me play in a college game, and tying Miami University (our rivals) while having an undefeated conference season.

At the end of the successful fall semester of his sophomore year, Les made what seemed to be a spur-of-the-moment decision that took him in an unexpected direction.

Now the unexpected happened that totally changed everything. My brother was in the army in Germany, and he urged me to join too. He said, "Bro. Come on over here. Germany is just like Hawaii." I figured, "He's pulling my leg! He's never been to Hawaii!" But I thought about it. One day, I went in the post office. The recruiter said, "Have you ever thought about joining the army?" When I asked what I had to do, he said, "Go up to Columbus and take the test." I said, "Okay." I went up to Columbus, took the test, and passed.

I came back to OU. Then I hiked back home, borrowed my Dad's car, packed up my stuff, and went home again. The coach, Carroll Widdoes, called me and asked, "Have you signed the papers yet?" I answered, "No, Coach." He said, "Well, don't sign them. Just come on back." I explained, "I have made a commitment. I have to honor it." He said, "Well, think about it. In three years, if you still want to come back to college, your scholarship will still be here."

Les spent three years in the army, and as he says, "I was over there in the army playing football and running track." When he got out, he returned to Ohio University.

The day I got out of the army in 1957, I contacted Coach Widdoes. I got out of the army on Wednesday, and I was back in school on Friday. When I first came back I ran spring track. When I came back in the fall I went back on the football team. Coach Blosser came up to me one day and said, "Les, you don't have a scholarship, you have the GI Bill." I said, "Okay," and went on and practiced that day. A couple of days later, Coach Widdoes came up to me and said, "You're back on scholarship. Forget what Coach Blosser told you." I went back to my scholarship, but I still had my GI Bill. I was able to help other students to get loans that they never had to pay back. My scholarship money and the GI Bill went to help other people.

We had a new young track coach [Stan Huntsman] when I returned to school. Using more up-to-date and modern training methods, my track accomplishments went up and up. Running against top-notch competition made me, and the team, better. OU was running with "the big boys" around the country, competing in Pennsylvania, Wisconsin, Texas, Iowa, and on many other major college campuses. We held our own too, beating some of the "biggies" along the way.

The 1958 football season was nothing to write home about, but we won more than we lost. In track we had a much more successful season, just missing out on winning the MAC championships. Personally I had a few accomplishments that still stand out in my mind. In the 1958 MAC track championship meet, I defeated a 1956 Olympian in the 200 meters in a time of 20.8 seconds—a record that stood for twenty years or more. In the NCAA trials that year, in Berkeley, California, I broke and set a new NCAA record for the 200 meters at 20.7 seconds, which made the national news. I also defeated a sprinter from Michigan University who was undefeated up to that point. Another high point was having my mom down for Mother's Day weekend to see me and our team compete in a meet. She said I shouldn't run so fast because I might hurt myself.

The 1959 spring track season turned out to be the best ever for me. I was drafted by the Baltimore Colts; I became the first OU runner to make All-American by placing third in the 200 meters in the NCAA finals; and I made AAU (Amateur Athletic Union) All-American again by placing in the top three in the 200. I graduated absentee while on the NCAA/AAU track trip. It had taken from 1952 to 1959, but I had done it in four years.

These accomplishments earned me a quick European trip and a spot on the 1959 United States Pan American [Games] team. I placed second in the 200 meters, earning a silver medal. Now I had a decision to make. Should I stay in the job I had just started, try out for the Colts, or try for the 1960 Olympics? I decided on the Olympics and my company granted me a leave to train. With the help of Coach Huntsman and my company, I went to Rome to compete. As the finals started I was behind, but the next thing I remembered was crossing the finish line a couple of inches behind the winner and taking the silver medal in a time of 20.6 seconds. Standing on the podium and seeing the American flag being raised brought tears to my eyes. How proud and happy I felt for all the help along the way, the long, hard work, representing America, and having the love of my family and friends; it is still hard to put into words, even after fifty years.

A crowning reward came to me a few years later when I was honored by being inducted into the Ohio University Hall of Fame. I was the first African American, the first Olympian, and the youngest to be inducted. It was an even greater honor to have others look at some of my accomplishments while at OU and say I was the "inspiration" that gave them the will to succeed.

In 1979, members of the 1953 MAC championship football team, including Frank Underwood and Les Carney, began planning reunions. They were set "for the first home game each year." Frank remembers them fondly:

Coming back and being together with our old football buddies is just a great positive experience. Coming back gives me another opportunity to associate with Ohio University and see how things are going here. I like to be with my buddies. The administration, the athletic department, and others have always supported us well. The 1953 team reunions are always wonderful times. Reunions are big on my agenda. They energize me.

Les agrees:

Speaking about that 1953 reunion team, one year we came together. We saw the football game. We had dinner and then we started discussing what we could give back to the university that would be commemorative of the '53 team. That night, Duke Anderson, who was our team captain in 1953, and a few of the other fellows suggested that we could set up an endowment fund. We made a pledge of fifty thousand dollars. At that point we suggested that the pledge should cover a five-year period. We started contributing. I think we have met that goal and have exceeded it. That is one of the good gestures from the '53 football team.

Lemuel O. "Rip" Nixon, 1952–54

"Rip" Nixon, the fourth athlete among the early arrivers, had excelled on the basketball court at Pittsburgh's Westinghouse High School. He enrolled at Ohio University in the fall of 1952 to become the school's first "colored" basketball player. However, he left at the end of his second year, disillusioned and disappointed at the treatment he got from a member of the athletic staff. He did not return until years later, when Underwood persuaded him to attend a Soulful Reunion. In talking about his experiences, he notes both the positive—especially the establishment of a black fraternity on campus—and the negative experiences.

My overall experience at OU was a positive one. I recall there were thirty-two black students on campus between 1952 and 1954, and four of them were from Africa. We all bonded. David Byrd, Les Carney, Sylvester Davis, LaQueth Fleming, Charles Hefflin, David Jackson, Ted Jackson, Grant Latimore, Howard Nolan, Frank Underwood, Charlie Wilson, George West, and I were responsible for returning Phi Chapter of Alpha Phi Alpha fraternity to Ohio University, which should be recognized as historic. There had not been enough black males prior to our attendance to maintain a chapter.

I know that some black students experienced discrimination at OU. Besides the well-known exception of the black barber, who would not cut our hair until after his shop closed, I didn't. My race problems were on the basketball road trips. For example, we played Miami of Ohio and stayed in Hamilton, Ohio. Coach Snyder distributed the postgame meal money, and six of us went to have our dinner. After going into a restaurant, hanging up our coats and hats, and sitting in a booth (we dressed like businessmen back then: suits, white shirts, ties, overcoats, and hats; we were sharp) a waitress came to the booth with *five* glasses of water. She looked at me and said, "I'm sorry but my boss will not allow me to serve you!" I got up, put on my coat and hat, and left. To their credit, my teammates did the same. One Irish teammate wanted to go back into the restaurant and break it up. My parents had prepared me for just such a situation, and I explained to my teammates that I would probably be the one arrested and to let it go. We went to five more restaurants before we found a greasy spoon to serve us.

The Alpha Phi Alpha fraternity was reinstated at Ohio University in 1956 due to the efforts of several future members of the Soulful Bobcats. That year's members included: (*top row*) Wilson Graham, Sylvester Angel, John Smith, and Howard Nolan; and (*bottom row*) Albert Smith, Theodore Jackson, Grant Fletcher Latimore, and Reginald Haley. 1956 *Athena. Courtesy of the Mahn Center.*

The single negative aspect of my time at OU is also what caused me to leave and not return for fifty-six years. Charles Hefflin and I were recruited out of Westinghouse High School in Pittsburgh by an OU alumnus. Hefflin was a premier track athlete. I played basketball. We were promised room-and-board jobs for our freshman year and full athletic scholarships if we made our respective teams and our grades were good during our freshman year. We met both requirements.

Upon return to OU for our sophomore year, I asked Kermit Blosser, the athletic director, about my scholarship. He told me he had given out all the scholarships. I was angry and disheartened and never shared that disregard of our verbal contracts with anyone except my parents and Heff, who was in the same situation. I played basketball that year and was the first black varsity basketball player for OU.

Members of Alpha Phi Alpha dance with their dates. 1957 *Athena. Courtesy of the Mahn Center.*

Hefflin and I left Ohio University at the end of sophomore year. Heff transferred to the University of Pittsburgh, went to medical school, and became a very prominent doctor. In 1955 I was given a basketball scholarship to St. Francis University. We made the NIT (National Invitational Tournament) in 1958, my senior year. I was standing near the hallway leading to the locker rooms in Madison Square Garden when I was approached by Jim Snyder, OU's basketball coach. He asked me why I hadn't returned to OU. I explained what Kermit Blosser had told me. He wanted to know why I hadn't come to him. My rationale was that Blosser was the athletic director, Snyder's boss. Why would I go to Snyder for resolution? I had lost trust. In retrospect, I believe that Coach Snyder was a good coach and a good man. I was thinking of my future and not my past.

Alpha Phi Alpha members attending a Halloween party in costume (*left to right*): Dolly Mayle Thomas, Ronnie Dozier, Ricky Browner, and Etta Bailey Graham. 1957 *Athena. Courtesy of the Mahn Center.*

I graduated from St. Francis, was drafted, and played basketball in the army for almost two years. The Signal Corps team I played on won the Third Army Championship two years in a row. I made the All Army

Team my second year. I was hired by IBM in 1964, was the first black Office Products [Division] sales rep in Detroit, and had a very rewarding career. I am grateful for all of my experiences because they were continual learning experiences, providing me with a happy life. I am also pleased to have returned to Ohio University for the Black Alumni Reunion after so many years. Some things don't change! The bond is still there.

The 1953 Contingent

In the fall of 1953, five more future Soulful Bobcats became freshmen Bobcats: Dorothylou Sands, Marlene Smith Eskridge, Alice Jones Rush, Claire Nabors McLendon, and Howard Nolan. Each of the women chose a major that led either directly or indirectly to a career in education. The lone male of the group enrolled in Ohio University's architectural engineering program to become an architect.

Dorothylou Sands, 1953–54 and 1957

Dorothylou, to whom this book is dedicated, was like her predecessors, Les Carney and Rip Nixon: she left Athens and Ohio University after a few semesters. Like Carney, she did return, at least for a while; like Nixon, she left without earning a degree. For her it was not elective military service or the disappointment of being denied a promised scholarship that caused her to leave school, not once, but twice. Her difficulties were caused by an undiagnosed medical condition.

I am the only child of Dorothy and Louis Sands; hence my name: Dorothylou. I am the fourth generation on one side and third generation on the other to be born in Pittsburgh, Pennsylvania. I grew up and attended Roosevelt High School in Dayton, Ohio. All of my extracurricular teen activities happened outside of high school. I belonged to The Orchidettes–Y-Teen Club, Al-Ka Pals, and the Young (Episcopal) Churchmen. I believe I held an office in all three organizations.

I worked at Wright-Patterson Air Force Base after I graduated in 1952. In August of 1953, my father asked me if I wanted to go to college. He gave me $450 from his endowment insurance policy. I applied to Miami University in Oxford, Ohio, but there were no rooms available. I had to go to a state school, so I decided on Ohio University. I knew Howard Nolan was a student there and that Marlene Smith [Eskridge] was enrolled for the coming year. At least I would know someone.

Friends of my parents drove me to Athens with all my stuff. I was the first of three roommates to arrive at Bryan Hall. Marlene [Smith] came later that afternoon. Janice Whitley came a few days later. (As freshmen, we had to be there earlier.) The room was barely big enough for one person, let alone three. I would be surprised if three white students lived in a room that small before or since. A short, slim, very personable young lady had the room next door to ours. Her name was Edwina Banks. We called her Eddie. She had been ill in high school and so was a little older than we were. But she was upbeat, witty, and pleasant. She joked that she was going to major in chemistry because those classes were mostly male. She was generous and shared the care packages she received from her mother. She also let some of our "stuff" overflow into her room.

The first day Marlene and I went down to Logan's bookstore. The first black person we saw was Cornelius Hopper. He greeted us like he had known us forever. We learned that there were so few of us on campus that we spoke to each other almost automatically. There were a little over forty of us in September 1953. I do not believe there had ever been so many females on campus.

There were a few parties at one of the married veterans' apartments in Vets Village. You did not need an invitation. You knew you were invited if you were black. The Alpha Phi Alpha fraternity had been affiliated with Ohio University since the turn of the century. In 1953 there were enough pledges to become an active fraternity again. I rode to Ohio State to several parties with the future Alphas, and some of the Alphas from OSU came down to OU for the big formal dance at the Student Union that reactivated the chapter. Paul Alexander was one of them; his date stayed with us at Bryan Hall.

There were no particular racial incidents while living at Bryan Hall. The dorm was very friendly. "Ma" Kelly was our twenty-four-year-old housemother.

Dorothylou Sands and Sherman Robinson

We became close to Fay Broida and Marcia Grossman. Fay was our floor chairman so they had a larger room. My roommates and I also had a larger room for second semester, but it was still not big enough for the extra mattresses we brought in for Mother's Day Weekend. Faye and Marcia told me they would be away that weekend and I could stay in their room. I got settled on my mattress, and a white girl from across the hall said her room was crowded. She asked if she could share the room with me. I said OK. Just before we drifted off to sleep, she asked me why I was so friendly with the Jewish girls. I was sort of taken aback. I was born on a street in Pittsburgh that was 90 percent Jewish at the time. On a Jewish holiday there were only three of us left in our classroom. I knew that there was anti-Semitism but was amazed at her asking me that question.

There were only four African American women in our dorm of 200, and we were nothing alike in size or shape, so we were amused when people mixed us up. One time when one of us was in the restroom someone asked, "Which one are you?" Then, whenever we were in the restroom and another one of us came in, we would ask, "Which one are you?" and laugh. We also had somewhat of a problem because Janice straightened her hair often, and she did not want Marcia to come in at that time. Eddie used a password if the door was shut, but Marcia was in our room so often that we finally gave up. She wanted to know if using a hot comb hurt your head.

I thought the dorm food was good. At dinner on Wednesdays and Sundays we had to wear stockings and blouses—no sweaters or bobby socks. On Sundays at noon, the dining tables had white cloths. Sunday evenings just a few

Soulful Bobcats

of us ate. We had soup, potato chips, dessert, and leftovers from the noon meal. I think we were one of the few state schools that served a Sunday evening meal, and I was amazed at the food that was consumed by the young men who worked in the cafeteria. We often ate with a Chinese girl from Hong Kong. Mingette Yin and her Puerto Rican roommate kept us laughing.

At the end of the semester my presence was requested at the Registrar's Office. Janice, as a senior, had the privilege of choosing her roommate and chose Marlene. They had to break one of the university rules and put me in a room with a freshman the next year. I was given Yvonne Spottswood's address, and we wrote to each other over the summer.

In September of 1954, my mother was ill, so just my father and I rode down to Athens. Janice, Marlene, and I had requested to live in the new dorm, Voigt Hall. The first floor was not finished when we arrived. My father and I got to my room and interrupted a bubbling young lady's cheerful conversation. It was Mitzi Eskridge, who was visiting from Howard Hall, the dorm next door where we would all eat our meals.

There were at least twenty more black students enrolled at Ohio University in 1954. Frances [Ramsey] became my other roommate. We both felt we knew each other as Joan Washington had talked about each of us to the other. Joan spent the winters in Tuskegee with Frances and the summers in Dayton with her father.

Though Dorothylou was enjoying life at the university, she found it difficult to handle some of her courses. She had undiagnosed narcolepsy, which made her fall asleep in classes. Her grades began to suffer.

I may not have been aware of many racial problems at OU as my mind was on a personal problem that influenced my life even more. I have had narcolepsy since I was twelve years old. Most people, including doctors, were not aware of this sleeping disorder at the time. I am certain I was put in English class because I did not score very high in our initial exams. I got a "C" in the class, which was needed to pass. Many of the other classmates failed, so I guess I didn't do too badly.

I slept until twenty minutes before the class started. I managed to make it across the street and into class on time. With a great deal of effort I made it until the end of the class without falling asleep. In biology class (I took it twice) we had a lot of slide lectures. As the lights went out, so did I. The Home Economics–Child Development classes I took were more active and probably more interesting; I did much better. I had a project for my Family Living class that I finished the day before it was due. I turned it in right away. The next day the professor could not find it. She gave me a "C" because it was not in on time.

I had a family class in which I was the only black person. We were told that a large part of our grade would be from our verbal participation. I was on a panel discussing mixed marriage. I used information and documents given to me by Marlene Smith, concerning her brother and his German wife. I got a 90 on my final, but a "B" in the class. There were several white girls in class that I had gone to high school with. The grades were posted. I had a higher test score but got a letter grade lower than they did. I was really counting on that grade. I needed a 2.0 to stay at OU. I believe I had a 1.99 or something close to it.

Dorothylou left Ohio University at the end of fall semester of her sophomore year. She went back to work at Wright-Patterson AFB.

I worked at Wright-Patterson AFB between 1955 and 1957 to save money to return to the university. To bring up my grades, I took a correspondence course in children's literature. I returned to OU in February 1957. I switched my major from child development to elementary education. I had to take a design class that was very similar to the one I took in child development. The teacher used my work as examples for the rest of the class. He gave us ideas on how to compile our work, making a portfolio. Again, I needed at least a "B" in this class. I had a "B" when I did the final project. He gave me a "C," which brought down my "B." I asked him why he gave me that grade. His answer was that he was a graduate student and couldn't give too many "A"s and "B"s. As the semester progressed, I realized that my narcolepsy was not going to permit me to do much better.

I had saved enough money for school to be able to go to California from Athens. I spent the summer looking for a job while receiving letters from Eddie and a few others, encouraging me to come to Cleveland for their OU party. They were planning to top the party we had had in Dayton the summer before. I flew to Chicago, went by train to Cleveland, and with Gayle Buckner, Douglas Farris, and Howard Nolan to Columbus, and then on the bus to Dayton.

I stayed in Ohio for three years and then returned to Los Angeles. A girl I met suggested that I see a doctor about my narcolepsy. He was the first doctor I had seen that put a name to my sleeping problem. He prescribed Ritalin, which I have taken ever since. In recent years I have attended several narcolepsy conferences. Now there are new medications, sleep centers, and universities such as Stanford that are doing research on the condition. My biggest problem was convincing people that I had no control over falling asleep.

I was not involved in civil rights activities. I guess I got all that out of my system writing letters complaining about the segregation that people were dedicated to keeping at Roosevelt High. I continued to write letters that were published in *Black Call* (an LA City College newspaper), *LA Times*, and *Ebony*.

I worked almost thirty years in various offices at Susan Miller Dorsey High School. The majority of my bosses understood my occasional sleep problem. I never stopped taking classes at one of the LA city colleges. I got an Adult School Credential in typing and sewing, though I never used it. I also took photography at Crenshaw Adult School from 1974–79. I also got a degree in management in 1981. When I retired in 1991, I continued to do genealogical research: I traveled and did archival research in Pittsburgh; Frederick, Maryland; Washington DC; and Annapolis, Maryland. And, of course, you can't do genealogy without spending time in Los Angeles and Salt Lake City.

The best thing about my experiences at Ohio University was the people I met. They would not have been an important part of my life if I had not chosen OU.

Marlene Smith Eskridge, 1953–57

During her freshman year, Marlene Smith was one of Dorothylou Sands's two roommates. And though her early academic experience in an inadequate, segregated Tennessee school was different from Sands's, they both graduated from the same high school in Dayton, Ohio. At Ohio University, Marlene chose a major in speech therapy and discovered her calling.

Attending an Alpha Phi Alpha party (*left to right*): Frank Underwood, Marlene Smith Eskridge, Charles Hefflin, Janice Whitley, and Grant "Fletch" Latimore.

As I begin to write this memoir, my mind is filled with memories of Ohio University and how I just happened to end up as an Ohio University alumna. I am a Tennessean and lived as a "Southie" until my sixteenth birthday. While a student during those lean years, the grade school teachers were teaching two or three classes in one room. Those men and women tried their best to give us a solid formal education. They all did all they could to see that we would be able to continue our education.

During the high school years, our classes included kids from neighboring towns. Two buses transported the students and, during the cold winter months, when the bus was in need of repair, my brother and I walked the two miles to school. Like most schools for Negroes, ours did not have the basic tools, such as typewriters, labs, sewing machines, and other necessities. Because this was not what my mother had envisioned for her children, I was blessed and was the one who was sent to a larger high school that transitioned me from a "Southie" to a Midwestern chick.

When I arrived at my Roosevelt High School in Dayton, Ohio, I had never seen such a large school in my life. I had heard that the "big city" school placed us "Southies" a grade behind. Well, the principal placed me in the college prep program. I actually performed well, with the exception of chemistry. Several of my teachers nominated me for the Honor Society, but due to the chemistry travesty, I did not quite make the cut.

My aspiration had been to attend the University of Michigan, but as my civics instructor said, "They will chew you up and spit you out." On the flip side of that sentiment, this instructor told his sister, who happened to be the dean's secretary at Ohio University, about me, and probably added that I was a "little ole country girl." That is how I ended up as an Ohio University alumna.

I arrived at Bryan Hall and met my two roommates. I knew one was from Dayton, and the other was from Cleveland. The Cleveland one even SMOKED! In fact it seemed like all the Cleveland girls smoked. The next few days were full of endless tests. I had never been tested for so many hours; my mind was going completely blank.

I met with my counselor, who said I was deficient in almost all areas. He added that I was not college material and that he could not understand my high rank at Roosevelt, which had been "A." During my first year, especially the second semester, I applied myself to my studies, which I really enjoyed, with the exception of math and chemistry. At the end of my second year, I proudly shared my grades with the counselor. As expected, he could not believe my success. My tenacity and hard work were due to the expectations of my family, who supported and believed in me. I could not let them down. I was the only child out of eight siblings to complete college.

18 Soulful Bobcats

Marlene Smith Eskridge. Eskridge was selected by Hugh Hefner, publisher of *Playboy* magazine, to be a member of Ohio University's Athena Queen Court. 1956 *Athena. Courtesy of the Mahn Center.*

Good times followed. I loved my major—speech and hearing therapy. My advisors, Dr. LaFollette, Dr. Wiseman, and Dr. Ham, were my surrogate parents. They believed I had a "special gift" that was meant to be shared with the world. Dr. LaFollette introduced me to all his colleagues at every convention. My fellow "Speechies" were inquisitive. They asked me racially based questions and, like all us students of color, I answered with candor and a matter-of-fact attitude. To my pleasant surprise, my "Speechies" later gave me a bridal shower.

During my junior year I was selected to represent my sorority, Alpha Kappa Alpha, on the Athena Queen Court. Hugh Hefner chose the winners, and when I was selected, of course I was quite surprised. The white students congratulated me as the promenade crossed the OU campus. To add to my experience, I was also pinned an Alpha Sweetheart. (My children would always ask Reggie and me what was happening in the picture the night he pinned me.)

Another fond memory occurred when my good buddy, Elva Jane Johnson (EJ), and I were asked to have cocktails with a photography professor, his wife, and a noted linguist. The linguist was extremely interesting to me due to our mutual love of communication. EJ and I often wondered why we were asked to join this entertaining group.

After graduation, Dr. LaFollette scheduled an interview for me for a summer job. The location of this teaching gig was in the southern part of the U.S. However, since I was married to Reginald Haley, an OU alumnus, I declined the offer. Once again Dr. LaFollette intervened and wrote a letter of recommendation to the assistant superintendent of Dayton Public Schools. During the interview, I was asked my thoughts on teaching white children. My response was, "A child is a child, regardless of color." When I began to teach, I was always the only black on the faculty. After several years, I found out I was the "trial balloon" to determine how a black speech pathologist would be accepted by the white populace. God bless my OU communication professors for preparing me academically and emotionally for the real world.

So many experiences happened during my four years at OU. It was one of the happiest times of my life. Life after college was exciting too. I thought I knew everything about speech therapy, but I encountered more prejudice in teaching in various schools. At one school, I asked the principal for desks and chairs that were the appropriate size for little kindergartners. She looked me up, down, and sideways and threw out an insult for my having the nerve to ask for something better. Directly after that, I informed my supervisor of the principal's very disgusted response. Later the supervisor made an impromptu visit to my classroom; within a week of that visit, I got desks and chairs that were the right size for my little students.

Fast forward to the 1970s: my mentor and I saw the need for a better understanding of various language patterns, i.e., of black and Appalachian speech patterns. The development of a program was extensive, and it became a political issue. After that eye-opening ordeal, I was happy to return to teaching children.

During the years before that, I was blessed with three wonderful children. I started graduate school during their somewhat turbulent teen and twix-teen years. Although they were a challenge, my dear darlings came through for me, and I actually had their support. After finishing the required classes, I decided not to march at commencement, but my children insisted. Barbara Jordan was the commencement speaker.

During my career I was named Teacher of the Year at Parkway School in Plainview, New York, and Distinguished Educator in Newark, Ohio. My experience at OU played a large part in shaping my career and my love for teaching. I also owe a lot to my parents and family for sending me away to receive a good education and the opportunity to interact with a diverse group of people. I almost forgot to mention: two of my three children, Kim and Reggie, are also proud graduates of Ohio University.

Alice Jones Rush and Claire Nabors McLendon, the final two female Soulful Bobcats to enter Ohio University in 1953, were both from Cleveland, Ohio. Both of them became teachers; Alice spent her career in the Cleveland Public Schools. After a stint in the same system, Claire moved on to Chicago, where she both taught and served as an administrator.

Alice Jones Rush, 1953–57

I was born in 1936 in Cleveland during the later years of the Great Depression. My parents divorced when I was about three years of age. My mother and I moved in with my grandparents, aunt, and roomers into a large middle-class home. There, I was raised in a comfortable, loving environment. I did very little outside our "colored" neighborhood. In school I excelled and received good reports. I was a scout, took piano lessons, and acted in plays at a community center and church.

All of this changed for me when my mother remarried and I moved into an integrated neighborhood out of my comfort zone. I no longer excelled and found my teenage years difficult. For the first time I experienced prejudice. Not even the high school counselor offered encouragement to me or many others of my race. We were not encouraged to go to college.

I turned seventeen two months before graduating from high school. On a beautiful spring weekend, I visited a friend of my mother's who was attending Ohio University. As I arrived at Lindley Hall, I witnessed students hanging out of Chubb Library's windows and sitting on the grassy knoll across from Lindley Hall. It seemed to me that college was going to be fun. It was then that I made my decision to go to this beautiful place.

In September 1953, I entered Ohio University. As an only child I had not experienced living with others or sharing. This was an exciting, difficult time adjusting to college life. I went from prejudice in high school to the same situation in college. There were approximately eleven black female students and perhaps thirty black males, including the African students, on campus. I had been warned that I would have to work twice as hard as the white students to make passing grades. Adjusting was slow. After about six weeks, I was called to what I call a "dummies" class meeting. Realizing that going home in embarrassment was not an option, I became a more serious student.

I remember being in a psychology class where the professor told a racial joke. I remember a science class in which the professor made me feel that I was too stupid to comprehend the material he presented. I was humiliated, embarrassed, and so upset that I called my mother at work in Cleveland. She worked for the United States Army. I do not know who paid for that phone call. There was also a time when we had to draw for our rooms in a lottery. I did not draw a room and would have had to find a room in Athens had my mother not interceded. Being a black young lady in the dormitory was difficult at times because it was hard to keep our hair neat, clean, and straightened. During those days, black women used straightening combs. We would roll up wet towels at the door of our rooms so that the odor of "hair frying" would not permeate the hall.

In June 1954, Ohio University's Board of Trustees unanimously agreed "that all freshmen students be housed in university housing, unless they are residents of Athens, or Athens County and commute daily, or have permission from one of the personnel deans to live with relatives." At the same meeting President Baker explained to the trustees "that the negro students live in university dormitories and they are served in all but two restaurants in Athens, but at present they are not permitted the use of the barbershop facilities in Athens."

I now realize the value of the black family we unknowingly formed on campus. We laughed, cried, and partied together. Some of us fell in love. I did not realize how much we meant to each other and the significance of the era we lived in until about 1991 when a classmate, Dorothylou Sands, brought us together for the first Soulful Reunion. It was then that I actually took time to remember and appreciate my experiences at OU.

I had been educated in and out of the classroom. There were people whom I had not thought about, such as my critic teacher. I thought of her kindness during a difficult time for me. I remembered Dr. Baker walking across campus, cheerfully speaking to us. I remembered going to the MIA movies on Fridays. I remember attending and getting autographs from the great Count Basie when his band was there to play for a campus dance. It was at OU that I developed my love for jazz. I remember the married veterans from the Korean Conflict living in Vet Village. It was a good place to relax and party. I had one job while I was on campus as a switchboard operator at Lindley Hall, making fifty cents an hour. I also remember walking to the black Baptist church on Sunday mornings. I remember the joy of my mom visiting for Mother's Weekend.

In September 1957, I began my thirty-year teaching career in the Cleveland Public Schools. This was a time when the Cleveland school system began hiring many black teachers. We were assigned to schools in the predominantly black neighborhoods of the city. As a child educated in this system, I can remember no more than three black teachers. I was in the classroom during the civil rights movement. I joined the NAACP and tried to instill pride in my black students and teach them to celebrate our ancestors, who had made great sacrifices for us. I married Roscoe Rush in February 1963. We raised two wonderful children.

During my years at OU, I took organ lessons in the music department. I have used this skill since graduation and continue to this day as organist at my church. I also became a member of Alpha Kappa Alpha sorority. It is the same sorority that we attempted to form at OU. We had first to establish a local sorority for two years. I remember doing a service project at the state mental institution. That is what AKA is about, being of service to others. I know that my years at OU prepared me to relate to people of all races and to contribute in a small way to the betterment of mankind. I am a proud graduate of OHIO UNIVERSITY.

Claire Nabors McLendon, 1953–57

I was Claire Nabors, a student from John Adams High School in Cleveland, Ohio. John Adams was about 20 percent African American, with many ethnics (Hungarian, Italian, and Slavs) from working-class families. My family consisted of my parents, my older brother, and me. Among my many activities were Service League, the marching band, the newspaper staff, the dance club, honor study hall officer, and homeroom president. In June of 1953 I graduated. A friend, Beryl Hannon, was a junior at Ohio University when I received a full tuition scholarship ($120) for my freshman year. My brother was also in college during my first two years at OU, and a scholarship helped my family with expenses.

When I arrived in Athens, there were about thirty-five black students: ten women, about twenty African American men, and five students from Africa. During the first week of school, my roommate and I were surprised to find students who had never seen an African American before. Somehow I felt

Members of Kappa Alpha Alpha sorority, in 1956, included: (*top row*) Frances Ramsey, Edwina Banks, Shirley McWorter, and Jean Palmer; (*middle row*) Dolly Mayle, Gloria Walker, Claire Nabors, and Eleanor Christian; and (*bottom row*) Marlene Smith, Barbara Ellis, Joan Washington, and Alice Jones. Another member, Mitzi Eskridge, is not pictured. 1956 *Athena. Courtesy of Mahn Center.*

the need to join organizations on campus to represent my race. I joined the Women's Glee Club, the Canterbury Club, and the choir at the Church of the Good Shepherd. The church became a comfortable place for me. When I was president of the Junior Dance Club, we went on a tour of Ohio colleges, including Antioch, where there were students whose dress and manner were unusual.

In the spring of 1954, Beryl Hannon Dade, Mary Raby Stafford, Jean Davis, and I went to Institute, West Virginia, to meet with Mrs. Gwendolyn Goldston, who was regional director for Alpha Kappa Alpha sorority. She said that there

18 Soulful Bobcats

Although Kappa Alpha Alpha was awaiting permanent residence and national affiliation, the sorority participated in a number of campus and community activities. 1956 *Athena. Courtesy of the Mahn Center.*

were not enough African American women on campus to draw membership from and that maybe a local organization might be a good beginning for us. So we began Kappa Alpha Alpha, a local interest group. We competed in many Panhellenic events, such as Siglympics, but we had an uphill struggle to win any of these events because we were only twelve, while other sororities had forty or fifty members to draw from. In the spring of 1956, we participated in the May Sing in Memorial Auditorium, and in May 1957, we had our first faculty tea. After we had been a local sorority for three years, the Panhellenic Council suggested we apply for status as a chapter of Alpha Kappa Alpha. During these years, we enjoyed many Alpha Phi Alpha parties, which were held at the Knights of Columbus Hall on the edge of town. They were fun, but arranging transportation was always an issue. It was not until 1956 that parties given by Alpha Phi Alpha were held on campus at Putnam Hall.

First semester of my senior year was spent with Alice Jones Rush and Jean Palmer McGee student teaching in Cleveland. (There were not enough places around Athens for student teachers.) On the way back to Athens for Homecoming, we had a flat tire and the first experience of changing a tire by the side of the road. After graduation in June 1957, Alice, Jean, and I "went over" at the Alpha Omega Chapter of Alpha Kappa Alpha in Cleveland.

I taught in the Cleveland Public Schools until 1961 when I got married and moved to Fort Sam Houston in San Antonio, Texas, where my husband was stationed. After six months there, my husband was discharged and we moved to Chicago. I taught in the Chicago Public Schools, spending most of my career in a small elementary school in Hyde Park-Kenwood near the University of Chicago. After teaching third grade for some time, I began work on a master's degree from [the] National College of Education [at National Louis University]. Included in my program were courses in special education, learning disabilities, and administration and supervision. I taught learning disabilities and later became assistant principal. During this time, I took courses at Chicago State University and became a certified counselor.

Always active, I joined Chicago Focus, the board of the Chicago area Girl Scouts, the Junior Governing Board of the Chicago Symphony Orchestra, and Jack and Jill of America; I also served as president of the Chicago Elementary Assistant Principals Association, and I am currently president of the Chicago Chums, Incorporated.

My oldest son was six weeks old when the March on Washington occurred. I was not able to go but baked cakes to be included in box lunches for those who did attend. Many of my family members—my parents, my brother, my youngest son, and a cousin—were all involved in politics. So I inherited some political parts. I went door-to-door canvassing for Model Cities program in the Woodlawn area, and I did office work at the McGovern headquarters.

Howard Nolan, 1953–57

Howard, along with Dorothylou Sands, Marlene Smith, Alice Jones, and Claire Nabors, arrived in the fall of 1953 and quickly bonded with the other African American students on campus. Like them, he was determined not to let his minority status and Ohio University's "somewhat of a hostile environment" stand in the way of achieving his goals. And his goal, in the 1950s, was assumed to be virtually unattainable for a colored man.

I had a very supportive mother and father at home. They had seventh-grade educations. They were from Georgia, and they had come north for opportunities to work and raise their kids in an environment where they could get a better education than they would have received in Georgia. I didn't realize that most of my friends and neighbors did not have that kind of supportive home environment. I was fortunate in that way. I also had very supportive teachers in grade school and in high school.

I almost went to Harvard. It would have been on a Naval ROTC scholarship, but the navy wasn't having any of me. They kicked me out because of a physical disability. Supposedly I had a heart murmur and flat feet to the third degree with bulges. They looked at my test scores, turned red, and assured me, "You'll find some place to go to school." So I ended up at Ohio University because it had an architectural engineering program in those days. I had decided about seventh or eighth grade that I wanted to be an engineer or an architect. People asked, "Do you know any architects?" I would simply reply, "No, I don't know any." "Then, why do you want to be one?" And I would say, "I don't know, I guess I want to be the first one."

You have to understand; it's difficult to explain to younger people how our society was in the 1950s. Yes, we had endured a war and people had fought and everything else, but things had not changed much. The South was rampantly segregated, and the North was subtly segregated. My marching out and proclaiming, "I want to be an engineer," made people stop and reflect. Even the dean of my college, where I was the only black student, said, "But there is no room for you! You are going to have to be a superman in order to be accepted into that career field."

Several future Bobcats at the Military Ball, February 23, 1957. Attending were (*left to right*): Leroy Massie, Helen Winfield, Carl Walker, Frances Ramsey Walker, Howard Nolan, and Joan Washington Nabors.

It was a constant test of my ability to endure and sustain myself in the face of people who would say, "It's just too soon. You should be patient. You should wait." Of course, I don't call myself arrogant. I just was determined. I couldn't wait. People would say that things would have to change, but I built my college career and my life career by saying, "I'll be an agent of that kind of change." I was blessed and I was able to be an agent of that kind of change. I was able to persevere when people put up hidden obstacles. I had to either give in to those obstacles or allow them to make me a stronger person.

18 Soulful Bobcats

Here at OU there was no blatant racism unless you were downtown and tried to go into certain bars and things like that. That's another whole story. [See Carl Walker's story about a scary incident in an uptown bar.] The speech thing was a problem.

I had one situation where I thought that I wasn't being graded fairly, and that led to the only meeting I had with the dean of my college. The situation was resolved because I needed to have that grade improved to raise my GPA so I could go ahead and get my degree. (I did not learn until I was about halfway through my engineering degree that students came to college to be taught what professors knew, and that they should spit this knowledge back to professors in order to pass. Students were not expected to think outside the box, nor to be innovative, because they would clash with the professors and not get good grades.)

In this situation, the problem about my grade was resolved, but at the end of the conversation, (I won't name names) but the professor, who stuttered awfully and who taught a course that no one took until he was at the end of his degree program, said, "You people have a speech problem. In addition to things that we have discovered here, you need to take an in-depth speech course." I had already taken the basic speech courses required by my program. I thought to myself, "It's me against them. I'm going to do it. I'm going to take the course that he is recommending. I won't explode."

I've always thought I spoke rather well. I took the speech course. You can call it arrogance if you want to, but I refused to write my speech until I started walking up the stairs from East Green where I lived to the speech building. A result of those impromptu speeches is that I achieved five hours of "A." It taught me a vital lesson in life. You don't get mad. You get even. He tossed lemons at me, and I made lemonade. That lesson has taught me you have to win friends and influence people if you want to get ahead. You have to make people think well of you in order to have them do business with you. That was the only time in my life that my speaking capabilities have been challenged.

One reason Howard and his Ohio University cohort were able to succeed at the university was because, as he says, "We were part of each other's support systems."

We who were here during the fifties congregated together. We met together in the student union, but we seldom had classes together. I was the only African American in the engineering college. Except for my roommate, I went for weeks without seeing other African American students. In saying that we were part of each other's support system, I mean that we grew together out of mutual needs. I guess that is human nature. You want to have friends and people to talk to. When somebody weakened and was asking, "What do I do? What do I do?" we sat down and talked with each other and strengthened each other.

I had so many varied experiences while on campus. I was what they called a campus activist. Our civil rights movement started before the civil rights movement. I started in our efforts to get haircuts here in town from the barbershops and in achieving access to the bars that we really didn't want to go in. I guess my biggest triumph was not necessarily when I was on campus but when I graduated. After five years at OU and almost five years in the air force making the world safe for democracy, in countries that didn't particularly want democracy, I was able to work in the highway department designing bridges. Then I was able to start my own company.

I have talked about some of the "bad times" on campus. But we had some good people—some people along the way who helped us get established at OU. As a result of some of the things that we had done, both here on campus and in other places, out of the clear blue, seemingly, President Ping asked me to become a trustee. Looking at it from a business standpoint, it was bad business, because we [his company, Moody and Nolan] weren't going to be able to work at Ohio University while I was on the board. My partners kind of opposed it. I related this to Dr. Ping, saying that if I became a trustee I wouldn't be able to work at OU for nine years. He said, "Howard, if you don't become a trustee, you'll never work for Ohio University again." I finally realized what an honor I was being given, to even be asked. That is something that a lot of people ask for and never receive. When I was finally sworn in and realized that the dean who had told me I had to be a super engineer in order to make it in my field was still living and was aware of my appointment, I think that was one of my quiet triumphs. I hold it dear.

Now one of the jewels on campus is the new Baker Center. It is a design of Moody-Nolan, which is the architectural firm I helped found. The challenge wás expanding on the needs of the students and making the union so user-friendly that it would become a gathering place. We opened the building up to the West Green and to the main campus, and we used some of our early library projects to create the mall concept that works really well.

We have on the Moody-Nolan staff a very strong historical preservation designer who also attended OU. That's why the new center fits into the campus setting so well. We achieved two things here. We satisfied a need, but we satisfied our client, OU. During the planning stage and throughout the process, it was important to get our client's thoughts. We put those thoughts into the building; the client went out and told friends how great we are.

I think that Ohio University has been good to me and that I have been good to Ohio University. I'm an honest person. Sometimes I may not sound as if I am, but I am. Here they teach you to learn. They plant a seed in you that tells you that you are somebody important. As people try to understand black reunions, why we keep coming back, it's that seed that is difficult to explain.

This [the Soulful Reunion] has been a unique experience in all our lives, but as we have our separate "Soulful Reunions" over time, we are going to squeeze them in with OU's reunions. The reception this year was absolutely tremendous. The younger folk declared, "We had no idea of the things you did and the way things were." I was honored last month by an organization I belong to. It was during Black History Month. I suddenly realized that, "Yes, I have made history. We've made history. We have made history here at Ohio University." Now we are determined to let people know what it was like when we were here. We want to give them some roots, some traditions to cling to. Everybody needs to know who they are and where they come from. If we can accomplish that, then the journey will have been worthwhile.

A 1954 Group

In May of 1954, the United States Supreme Court ruled in *Brown v. Board of Education* that separate but equal schools were not, and could not be, equal and therefore that segregation in education was unconstitutional. Five future Soulful Bobcats—Frances Ramsey Walker, Joan Washington

Nabors, Ejaye Johnson Tracey, Adger W. Cowans, and Carl H. Walker—
entered Ohio University in the fall of that year. This mid-decade group
was somewhat diverse: Frances and Joan had roots in Tuskegee, Alabama;
Ejaye and Adger were aspiring artists; Carl was older, a veteran of the
Korean War, and a transfer student. Of the five, Frances, who grew up in an
unusual educational setting, was the most directly affected by the Supreme
Court's decision.

Frances Ramsey Walker, 1954–58

As a black girl growing up in the middle of Alabama in the '40s and '50s, I came
from a different place, a different time, and different circumstance for any child,
white or black. My parents met as students at Tuskegee Institute and graduated
from college in 1925. Dad did his professional development at Cornell with his
master's in institutional management. Mom got her master's degree from
Tuskegee in home economics. It was unusual to have both parents have graduate
degrees in those days. The expectations were high for my two brothers and
me. Both of my brothers have earned doctorate degrees, and I achieved the
level of Specialist in Early Childhood Education. After my parents married they
moved to Chattanooga, Tennessee. My father opened a bakery, which he
operated successfully throughout the Depression. After the Depression was
over, he returned to Tuskegee to teach, feeling this would afford more security
to his family. He eventually became the director of the School of Commercial
Dietetics, Foods, and Nutrition and remained in that position until he retired.
My mother ran the campus savings and loan, which functioned as the black
bank in town. Because she worked there, we knew everybody in town.

I was born at John A. Andrews Hospital, a teaching hospital at Tuskegee
Institute, Alabama. Along with my two brothers, my family and I lived directly on
the campus of Tuskegee. All of my primary schools—the nursery, preschool, and
elementary schools—were university lab schools. My teachers were demonstration teachers with advanced degrees who directed student teachers and
taught education courses. My schoolmates were children of faculty members or
doctors and medical staff from the veterans hospital located nearby.

Dr. George Washington Carver was a mentor to my father. Since my dad was in foods and nutrition, every time Dr. Carver wanted to develop a formula for sweet potato flour or peanut meal, he and my dad would get together in my mom's kitchen and stir up all kinds of muffins and breads. Of course, my brothers and I would have to be the "tasters." Dr. Carver was a regular figure around the campus. You would see him pick up a twig or stick that had fallen from a tree. Several days later, you would hear that he had invented a new ink from pecan bark or something. I enjoyed visiting him in his museum/office. He was very patient, explaining the importance of the balance of nature. He taught me all about ecology before it was politically correct. My favorite place in his lab was his botany lab.

In addition to observing Dr. Carver on campus, Frances enjoyed the activities of the soon-to-be-famous Tuskegee Airmen, who trained there as a part of their military service.

Life in a small southern town in the '40s and '50s was about as bucolic as one could imagine. My memories from that time are of the Tuskegee Airmen and their impact on life in our town. Because of them, we acquired a fleet of taxicabs, diners, and three supper/night clubs. Many of the leading bands of the era came through to entertain the soldiers. I remember Lena Horne, Ella Fitzgerald, Duke Ellington, and Lionel Hampton made appearances. Many other dance and jazz bands came to the nightclubs as did USO shows. Little did I realize that I saw history in the making.

After the war was over, more students enrolled in Tuskegee, and the college grew in size and stature. We enjoyed all the school's activities as they changed through the seasons. The (black) Southern Intercollegiate Athletic Conference had their basketball tournament in February. The (black) National Medical Association had a biennial conference on campus. Spring brought the Food and Nutrition Show, which attracted eminent personnel and vendors from all over the country. It also meant track and field competitions between black colleges. Jesse Owens and Nell Jackson were Olympians who came out of such a setting. In summer, prominent tennis stars, such as Althea Gibson, would participate in tennis tournaments. Homecoming was the highlight of the fall season, with its floats and parades and balls. The Greek organizations had their lines in the fall and spring. I knew all the songs and chants of the various groups by the time I was in seventh grade. By paying five dollars per academic year, faculty members were granted admission to all plays, concerts, and entertainment on the campus. We could go to first-run movies on Wednesday and Saturday nights for only ten cents.

Even though Tuskegee is a small town, we enjoyed a rich and fulfilling life that allowed us to develop in a safe environment far away from the pervasive climate of hard-core racial segregation. At the time, public accommodations were marked "White Men," "White Ladies," "Colored Men," "Colored Women." My mother would not let us use public accommodations. We rode in private cars on trips to Atlanta and Montgomery, thus avoiding the experience of sitting in the back of the bus. We stopped and had a snack or lunch at a friend's house instead of subjecting ourselves to segregated lunch counters. Little did we recognize the efforts our parents and teachers made to protect us from the cold realities of life.

High school, however, was a rude awakening into the real world. The high school was a lab school to a degree, but it came under the auspices of the Macon County public school system. The teachers were master demonstration teachers, and, again, we had student teachers from the campus. The school maintained a high accreditation rating because we had access to the resources of the university. We had access to the library, the swimming pool, the tennis and basketball courts, and the stadium and football facilities. Our school was the venue for many statewide championship events, as segregated black schools simply did not have these kinds of resources.

Students at Tuskegee had to do internships and used the children in the Tuskegee community as their subjects. We were taught dance, swimming, tennis, and stagecraft. We received all the trappings of a private school and advantages that most black students were not privy to.

For the first time, we had to buy our own textbooks and materials. The books were secondhand and came from the white schools; some had pages torn out or answers written in the back. We bought them at Kresge's. They were only available during the first two weeks of school. If you lost yours during the year, you could not replace it. Being from Tuskegee, we could order books from the state repository in Montgomery. My brother had to order his Latin text from the state because the white students didn't have Latin classes.

Later in my teenage years, we interacted with college students, and many times we pretended to be college students ourselves. As a joke we tried to get them to make comments about our parents, whether they liked them as profs or not.

I played classical piano quite well. As a result, I found myself being the accompanist for the chorus and the unofficial pianist for all kinds of public meetings and functions. I wanted to be a majorette in the worst way, but every year I was elected "Miss Freshman" or whatever and rode on floats and cars instead of marching in the parade. I was the Homecoming Queen, so I got to sit with the football team on the field. After that, everyone thought I was the football captain's sweetheart.

Our parents taught us that we were products of their hard work and that we were to serve with humility. We were obligated to achieve and go out into the world to give back to our race what we had been given. We were to "Lift the veil of ignorance from our people," as instructed by Booker T. Washington, founder of Tuskegee. The academic standards and expectations for us were high; college and beyond were the destinations for us. I never knew you had a "choice" of going to college. The question was, where and what graduate school were you interested in? From this background, I assumed that I was ready for college.

My longstanding goal had been to attend Oberlin College in Ohio. I played classical piano, and I was going to major in music. As part of the admissions process I had to submit a juried audition, but that year my music teacher became ill and was not able to prepare me adequately for the audition. I did not pursue Oberlin any further. When I was in the eleventh grade, I had the opportunity to attend Fisk University's early admission program for academically advanced students. But since I was interested in music I did not attend. I was offered scholarships to Spelman and Talledega Colleges, but my parents felt that, if I was going to a HBCU, I might as well stay and go to Tuskegee. I wanted no part of that. I wanted to get as far from home as I could—thus, Ohio.

In June 1954, the landmark segregation case of *Brown v. Board of Education* changed educational opportunities for black students in Alabama. In an effort to keep them from attending white state universities, the Alabama Department of Education would pay the cost of tuition, room and board, and transportation to any accredited school in the United States if the subject matter were not taught at a black state college in Alabama. The challenge to become eligible for state aid was to find an academic discipline that was not covered by a major in education with a minor in a specific discipline. This was the determining factor in my being a student in the College of Arts and Sciences with a major in psychology. Being covered by "state aid" for most of my college expenses, I was not a profound financial burden on my parents.

When Frances arrived at Ohio University, she moved into the brand new, barely finished dormitory named for the former long-term dean of women, Irma Voigt; met other Negro students, including her future husband, Carl Walker; helped begin a sorority; encountered a new brand of prejudice; observed the cultural differences between white and black students; and gradually adjusted to college life.

So, in September 1954, I boarded the train by myself for Ohio. The eighteen-hour trip in the "Negro Section" required that I change trains in Cincinnati and take a train east to Athens in a mixed car. Arriving in Athens, I took a cab, instructing the driver to go to Voigt Hall in my very southern voice. He took me to Boyd Hall. I told him this was not the right place, that Voigt was a new building. He responded, "Lady, nobody lives in that place. It's not finished yet." My heart sank. What was I to do? I was 500 miles from home, and I didn't have anywhere to go. Eventually he drove me around to College Street. Sure enough, Voigt Hall was sticks and mortar and construction debris, but the residential part—the second, third, and fourth floors—were complete and functional. The lobby and basement were completed as the year wore on. When it was finished, the lavish décor was worth the inconvenience and wait. The front marble portico and white columns made me feel right at home.

That evening, Yvonne, Janet, Mitzi, and EJ, the girls from Howard Hall, and I set out to "check out" the student center. We found the fellows in the basement, playing a wild game of bid whist and shooting pool. We pranced back and forth several times until several of them decided to "hit" on us. This is my first

Frances Ramsey and Carl Walker attend the Voigt Hall Winter Formal.

recollection of meeting Carl Walker. Little did either of us realize that we would eventually become life partners.

That year I had two room-mates, Dorothylou Sands and Yvonne Spottswood. Yvonne was from Cincinnati. She carried a large academic load and had a board job, so I did not see much of her except at night. For senior year, she moved to the Student Union dorm and I moved to Welch Cottage. Dorothylou was a sophomore from Dayton. Since she had been at OU the year before, she knew everybody and all of the ins and outs of college life in Athens. Yvonne and I had the advantage of learning from her previous experiences, some of which were rather comical.

Residents of Voigt Hall ate next door at Howard Hall. Imagine running out in the snow and rain to go to breakfast on a Saturday or Sunday morning. I skipped a lot of breakfasts. It was the tradition to "dress" for Wednesday night dinner. We wore hose and heels and dresses instead of saddle shoes and bobby socks. There were white tablecloths on the tables, and meals were served family style as opposed to green plastic trays cafeteria style.

Voigt Hall was directly across the street from the student union. It was the standard thing to stay at the library and study until nine o'clock. Then we would

The new student center (later named for President John Baker) opened in 1953 and quickly became popular with both black and white students. 1955 *Athena. Courtesy of Dan Dry Associates.*

make a beeline for the student center and meet in the Bunch of Grapes Room. We would dance our hearts out until 9:45. I could dash across the street and be in the dorm before the 10:00 PM curfew. I have memories of Carl and me sitting on the wall in front of Voigt Hall, listening to Ted Jackson sing romantic ballads when he was performing for formal dances at the student center. Now songs, such as "Moonlight in Vermont" or "The Nearness of You," bring back memories of life on College Street.

One of the major adjustments I had to make was living in a dorm with white girls. I did not grow up with sisters, so the very idea of being constantly surrounded by people was a big adjustment for me. In addition, cultural differences are really brought out when you live in such an environment. The way non-blacks go about solving problems, their logic, attitudes about differences, religion, and marriage were constant sources of amazement to me.

The residents of Welch Cottage, 1958. Front row (*left to right*): June Cunningham, Marsha Heinz, Marjie Maley, Mary Alice Joslin, and Wanda Finley. Middle row (*left to right*): Toni Gentile, Myrna Weatherbee, Rose Turrin, Laverne Snyder, and Elizabeth Lou Moore. Back row (*left to right*): Maxine J. Hoyles, Connie McClure (Proctor), Fran Islay, Linda Tichy, Marlene Sabes, Mary Jo DeSantis, Marilyn Hill (President), and Frances Ramsey. 1958 *Athena. Courtesy of the Mahn Center.*

We black girls were there to get an education so that we could get jobs after graduation. The white girls appeared to be there to get husbands. Their pressure to be "connected" would start as early as "rush" freshman week. The "live or die" opportunity to join the right sorority determined your very being as a person or your success for college life. Your dating life among the elite fraternity men was shaped by which sorority you belonged to.

Although Frances may have been somewhat apprehensive about her living arrangements initially, she obviously took it all in stride and in her

Members of Kappa Alpha Alpha packing gift boxes for patients at the Athens Mental Hospital as part of their community outreach program. 1957 *Athena. Courtesy of the Mahn Center.*

senior year she and her new roommate Maxine Hoyles Yates were living in Welch Cottage, a much smaller and more intimate housing situation than Voigt Hall. The 1958 *Athena* included the following statement and photograph: "The seventeen girls living with their proctor in Welch Cottage were a happy family sharing in fun-making and helping each other work out little problems."

Black girls were not invited to be a part of rush activities. In the course of time, an interest group for AKA was started, and most of the black girls who were interested joined Kappa Alpha Alpha. Girls interested in Delta or the other groups went to Ohio State to pledge. The KAA group eventually gained a charter from the National AKA. Our KAA chapter was recognized on campus and became part of the Panhellenic Council. As our group's representative on council, I was able to see the inner workings of white organizations and how they function. I was able to observe the politics of it all. It is a life skill I carry to this day.

Another issue that confronted me for the first time was religious differences. I was accustomed to the idea of racial and ethnic differences, but I really was not prepared for the idea of religious differences. My family is composed of Episcopalian, Methodist, a Catholic, and a heavy dose of Bible-thumping Baptist.

Members of Kappa Alpha Alpha local sorority attend a faculty tea hosted by Miss Allyne Bane at her home in May 1957.

Yes, it is quite an ecumenical mix! Imagine my sense of awe when I would hear my dorm mates discussing why they would not associate with or date a person because of their religious persuasion. I grew up as a southerner who believed that as long as you go to church, you are a worthy person, regardless of the affiliation.

Frances was a psychology major in the College of Arts and Sciences where she usually performed well and sometimes surprised her professors.

My academic experiences at OU were not unduly challenging, except for French. My French teacher was a war bride. She perceived us as lazy crybabies. European students, in her view, were more disciplined. She proceeded to prove that by making the class as difficult as she could. I had her for four semesters, and I got my first "D" ever one semester in one of her classes. After my first two years of boring required core classes, my work became more exciting. Many courses were seminars as opposed to lectures. The civil rights movement was just beginning to take shape. I was constantly asked about segregation and being black in the South. Most students were Midwestern and had not experienced things outside the area. Few, if any, had interacted with blacks before coming to college. Ours was really an exchange of cultures in retrospect. I would tell them that, yes, the things that they read about and saw pictures of actually were true. People, both blacks from the North and others from around the United States, found it hard to believe that things like this happened in this country—that it was not fiction. The professors were more interested in my personal story and experiences than the students were. They were surprised to learn that black students at OU felt the ostracism of institutional racism that was present at the time.

One year my Dad was returning home from some postgraduate work at Cornell University. He came though Athens to give me a surprise visit. Yvonne and the gals from Howard Hall were bringing him to meet me as I came from class. As I met him on the sidewalk in front of the student center and let out all kinds of screams of joy, the dean of women, Margaret Deppen, was just behind me. She enjoyed my moment of bliss and teased me for quite a while afterwards for the way I acted. Dad was impressed to know I was in zoology lab until 5:00 PM and wasn't frittering away my time doing more pleasurable things.

My major advisor, Dr. Patrick, was chairman of the Psychology Department. When he met me for the first time, he had my freshman placement test results in front of him. He said he did not think I would place where I did because I had attended a segregated black school in the south. They had scheduled me for remedial classes and a speech assessment to improve my speech and articulation. I qualified for honors English, and I made an "A" in that required class. Somehow Dr. Patrick had heard that dad had dropped by to see me and that he was a professor at Tuskegee. Instead of counseling me about my coursework, he wanted me to talk about Tuskegee and Booker T. Washington. I had to tell him that I did not know Booker T. Washington personally; he was a little before my time. I think of Professor Patrick fondly; we remained friends for many years. He even sent us a wedding present when Carl and I got married.

Somehow, Carl discovered that I played piano. He has an undying love for classical music and history. We made dates to attend the symphony concerts on campus. That connection led us to studying and sharing much of campus life together. We became best buddies and really good friends, enjoying each other's company. I don't remember ever actually saying, "Yes," to him, but Christmas my junior year we became engaged. He had been a transfer student from West Virginia State, so he graduated two years before I did. He got a job as a social worker in Cleveland. He would come down to visit in Athens as much as he could. The fellows knew that I was "Carl's girl" and would not ask me out. As a result, my college life changed, and I became active in groups such as Panhellenic Council, Canterbury Club, and KAA sorority. I sang in the choir and became very involved in activities at the Episcopal church. I was a student representative to conferences of the Southern Diocese of Ohio.

Reflecting on the four years I spent at Ohio U, I feel that it was a very necessary part of my life. Being a liberal arts major, the skills I left with were not job specific. I knew that graduate school would be the determining factor that guided my career. But my experiences at OU were broad and taught me many useful life skills, including political and organizational skills.

For Frances, who became Mrs. Carl Walker soon after she graduated, the next years involved moving frequently, teaching in a number of different cities, and continuing her education in a variety of ways.

Graduation time in June arrived but was all a blur. I was busily engaged in planning my wedding. Things on campus were no longer significant to me. It was time to put college behind me and get on with our lives together. Carl and I were married in Tuskegee in 1958 and moved to Cleveland where we lived for one year. Being a graduate of Ohio University helped me get a job as assistant children's librarian quite easily even though I did not have training in library science. They recognized my credentials in liberal arts and accepted me.

As a married couple we relocated to several cities across the United States. Our first move after Cleveland was to Baltimore, Maryland, where Carl worked for the Social Security Administration and I took courses at Johns Hopkins to qualify for the National Teacher credential and taught fourth grade.

After three years in Baltimore, we moved to Washington, DC, where our son Kenneth was born and where I taught fifth and second grade. DC was an exciting place during the Kennedy years; we actually went to the March on Washington and heard the now-famous "I Have a Dream" speech.

Three years later we relocated to Dayton, then Detroit in time for the race riots, then to San Francisco at the height of the Black Panther Movement. A significant promotion for Carl brought us back to the east to Baltimore and, after five years there, we moved to Atlanta where we have been for thirty-seven years.

In Atlanta I grew professionally and also made good career advancement. I earned a master's degree from Oglethorpe University and did work on the ed specialist at Mercer University. On being hired for Fulton County Public Schools, I was told I was assigned to a school in an all-white, upwardly mobile gated community because, "I know how to talk like those people from up north." I stayed with Fulton County as a curriculum resource specialist until I retired in 2001.

One of the highlights of my career was to go to Oxford, England, to study the British Infant School system. I was also honored to be selected the Southeastern winner of the Excellence in Teaching award given by the National Council of Negro Women. One outcome of this honor was that all the recipients served as consultants to Dr. Dorothy Height. For two summers I went to Mount Holyoke College to attend sessions on developing mathematical thinking and ideas. I was also recognized as a Shell Oil Company Master Teacher for this work in math. I also became an Apple Core teacher, sponsored by Apple Computer Corporation, to teach computer literacy. I retired in 2001!

Joan Washington Nabors, 1954–58

Joan spent each school year between the ages of eight and eighteen in Tuskegee, Alabama, where she lived with her aunt and uncle and became Frances Ramsey Walker's best friend. She spent each summer with her father in Dayton, Ohio, where he was executive secretary of the city's Urban League and where she became friends with schoolmates Dorothylou

Sands, Marlene Smith Eskridge, and Elva Jayne Johnson Tracey. She enrolled at Ohio University because she had friends there, thought it was beautiful, and liked the fact that the small-town setting was similar to Tuskegee. Like Frances, she was involved in founding the forerunner of Alpha Kappa Alpha. She also became a teacher, opened a school, and eventually had a second career as a storyteller.

I was born in Minneapolis, Minnesota, and lived in Pittsburgh, Pennsylvania, for one year. Because of the death of my mother when I was eight years old, I moved to Tuskegee to live with my aunt and uncle. Tuskegee was my home until I went to college. Summers were mostly spent in Dayton, where my dad had moved to become executive secretary of the Dayton Urban League. Friendships were made with many, including Dorothylou Sands, Marlene Smith, and Elva Jayne Johnson. Years later Ejaye and I would follow Dorothylou and Marlene to Ohio University.

Beside the proximity to family and having friends who would be attending, Ohio U appealed to me because of its setting. It was a small college in a small town where most activities centered around campus life—much like the campus setting at Tuskegee. Frances Ramsey and I had been best friends throughout elementary and high schools at Tuskegee. However, it was a surprise to each of us when we learned that the other had also chosen to go to OU and that we could continue our close friendship through the next four years as well.

Our freshman class included the largest number of Negro (politically correct at that time) students ever to set foot on OU's campus. I believe the timing of our arrival, which coincided with the onset of the movement toward integration, gave all of us a particularly unique place in history: we were a group of Negro students attending a predominantly white college. It required that we become trailblazers, whether we expected to be or wanted to be. It also intertwined our lives forever. Years later, when we returned to Ohio University for our first Soulful Reunion, I asked John "Breeze" Smith why he thought our bonds were strong. He replied, "Because we had to struggle together."

My three roommates, Shirley Gates, Louise Tarrer, Sarah Harris, and I quickly settled into life at Scott Quad, where I would live all four years. Many of the students had never seen a black person, let alone lived near them. We fielded questions about skin color, hair, etc., and there were some girls who almost moved in with us! Nevertheless we enjoyed working with others and assuming dorm responsibilities. The four of us formed a singing group, The Darlings, and performed for groups all over campus. One of the highlights was our performance at the Rusty Bryant concert, sponsored by the Alpha Phi Alpha fraternity.

We formed the first black local sorority, Kappa Alpha Alpha, which later became the national sorority Alpha Kappa Alpha. I served as president for one year. Participation gave us another entrée into campus life; African American women were taking part in activities previously open only to the white women. For the first time, our sisters were in the running for Greek Week Queen. Hugh Hefner was the judge that year and selected Marlene Smith as first runner-up. In my junior year I was tapped to be a member of Chimes, the academic honor club. When we returned for our Soulful Reunion in 1991, I met Lois Thompson Green, who arrived at OU the year I graduated. She shared that she had seen my picture in the yearbook with Chimes members and had vowed that she would strive to become a member also. In her junior year she did become the second African American woman to be tapped. I hope there have been many more.

Although most of our experiences were positive, there were moments when prejudice and discrimination raised their ugly heads. Shirley McWhorter (African American) and Ida Mae Ryan (Caucasian) decided they would test the system and see what would happen if they applied to room together the following year. The policy was that upperclassmen could choose roommates and, whenever possible, the choice would be accepted. No one ever *said* anything about race. Both girls were called into the dorm mother's room, where they were told that the request was unusual and that Ida Mae's mother would have to be contacted. To which Shirley replied, "What about *my* mother?" Another incident occurred one night when we looked out the window into Scott Quad's courtyard and saw three girls dressed as Ku Klux Klan members on their way to a costume party! A trip to the dorm mother's room put a quick stop to that!

There were, however, situations when we were well aware that we were given preferential treatment. As freshmen, we *always* had Negro roommates

Ohio University coeds host Ohio State University coeds for a Homecoming football game. The group included Barbara Ellis Carney, Janet Lowe Bullard, Yvonne Spottswood Scott, Frances Ramsey Walker, and Mitzi Eskridge Johnson.

and we always had a room in the dorm. Only married students were allowed to live off-campus in the community. This was in complete opposition to the policy of earlier years. Several years ago I interviewed Mrs. Edwards of Dayton, who had attended in the 1940s. She said that Negro students at that time were not allowed to live in the dorms. And so they lived mostly on Washington Street, which was commonly known as Black Street.

Joan Washington Nabors and Leon Ward take a break, relaxing on the college green.

I graduated from OU in 1958 with a BS in child development and family living. I accepted a position as a preschool teacher in Highland Park, Illinois. I learned before I was interviewed that, not only would I be the only African American who taught there, I'd be the only one who *lived* there as well. (Trail-blazing 201!) There were people who were maids and mechanics, but they went home to Evanston and Chicago at night. I lived with a Jewish family, which provided me with a rich living, as well as working, experience.

It was in Highwood, Illinois, that I received my most dramatic experience of discrimination. I was refused service when I went to an Italian restaurant with friends my age. My friends were told by the manager that we had to leave since they didn't serve Negroes. I had been there with the family I lived with and with others, and nothing had been said. But this was discrimination *Northern* style: sometimes you could eat; sometimes you couldn't. It depended. The people in Highland Park rallied and boycotted the restaurant. When a soldier from a nearby base was also turned away, the restaurant finally had to close. Yea, for the home team!

I worked in Highland Park for three years and then married Chuck Nabors and moved to Salt Lake City, Utah (Trail-blazing 301!). Salt Lake is a beautiful city and in many ways is a wonderful place to live. But in 1961 it was as prejudiced as the Deep South. Nevertheless, we adjusted, found our niche, and raised our family: Brian, Kelley, and Matthew. Chuck taught at the University of Utah until his death in 1986. Although we sometimes considered returning to the East, Utah had become home.

Over the years I have worked in preschools, worked with young children with behavioral disorders, and supervised Head Start and daycare teachers. I completed my MS in early childhood in 1983. The same year, another teacher and I opened a school for fourth to eighth graders, which we ran for seventeen years. It was amazing and one of the most challenging experiences of my life. I returned to teaching Pre-K part-time and finally fully retired in 2007. For over thirty years I have been a storyteller, primarily of African and African American stories. This has now become my major career, and I work with schools, libraries, and at cultural events throughout the state. My partner and I released a CD of African stories two years ago.

My husband and I were both involved in civil rights and politics in Utah. I have continued my involvement, which has increased since retirement. I had the pleasure of campaigning in Colorado for Obama and being in Washington during the inauguration period. I serve on boards that are mainly involved with community and justice. Brian and I serve together in an organization that helps in Eritrea, Africa. We had hoped to visit there, but the country is not stable at this time.

Travel has been an important part of my life in recent years. I am fortunate to have a daughter who works for an airline, and it allows me to travel whenever and wherever I want. In Kenya I was able to gather stories and add them to my repertoire. Overall I see that my interests and involvement seem to have followed different paths along the way but have continued in the same direction. Ohio University served an important role in fostering those interests and guiding me along my life's path. And I am so grateful for the diverse experiences I encountered at OU that helped shape my world.

Ejaye Johnson Tracey, 1954–58

Ejaye grew up in a predominantly white section of Dayton, Ohio, where she and her brother felt like "aliens in a hostile land." Her high school was integrated but many teachers had racist attitudes. She longed to study art, fashion, and acting at university, but had to make a more practical decision to complete a degree in speech therapy. Eventually, however, she became the artist she wanted to be, acting on stage, in films, and on television, and finally working as a jazz singer in New York City.

I grew up in a home filled with love, laughter, books, smells of good cooking, bountiful Christmases, and music. In fact the soundtrack of music I hear in my head still permeates my meaningful experiences. As an only daughter, I didn't know I had an atypical black middle-class upbringing. That labeling would come much later, long after graduation from Ohio University.

I was born in Dayton, Ohio, to William H. Johnson and Mildred Keller Johnson, the first and only daughter of their three children. My parents were both professionals, although my mother didn't work until after her children were in school. My father was in social work, and my mother became a teacher after she earned a second degree in elementary education. (Her first degree in languages could not be used in the segregated city in which she lived.) They had met and fallen in love at West Virginia State College. They introduced us to a life that revolved around family and social activities and encouraged us to live up to our level best.

What was atypical about my family was that we lived in a section of Dayton in which most of the black population did not reside. Although my parents saw that we participated in our black church activities where I met other children of color, I grew up with mostly white playmates and classmates in an elementary school where my brothers and I were the only Negro children. We literally felt ourselves to be "aliens in a hostile land." Though we were happy children, we endured the pain of being different. My first day of kindergarten, while being enrolled by my mother, one new soon-to-be class-mate pointed to me and loudly asked his mother if I was a "nigger." It was my introduction to the word, and I heard it more often than I care to remember in the years to follow. Not used affectionately, it was more scalding to me than being turned away from a downtown theatre by a red-faced box-office attendant who refused to admit me and my mother to the movie, *Snow White and the Seven Dwarfs,* because we were "colored." This was baffling to me, as my mother had combed out my pigtails and curled my hair, put me into my best dress, and allowed me to wear my patent leather Mary Jane shoes!

Through elementary school, it was more apparent that I could only be tolerated and not necessarily accepted by most of the white children and teachers. My protective family life shielded me as much as possible from the barbs of a hostile world in which I found myself. Despite being "special and different" from the norm expected from a colored child, I paved the way for my brothers. I often had to physically fight for them, help them hide, or run home to keep from being beaten and bullied. (When we ventured into the black neighborhood, we also were chased and bullied.) We were always proving ourselves.

At home there was pressure on me to maintain high grades and behave properly despite these battles. I carried this stress in numerous ways. My parents expected me to excel and pushed me in areas where I showed particular talent. Some of my white teachers may have encouraged my artistic and academic talents, but I was always aware that I should not "outperform" my white classmates. (My "A"s often had a minus sign attached, whereas other less gifted received the "A" or "A+.") I worked seriously to be popular and excel in my grades.

Homework was completed near my father's chair, where he read several newspapers and magazines while smoking his pipe or daily cigar. We listened to Edward R. Murrow, "Amos and Andy," and "Your Hit Parade" on radio. We listened extensively to Daddy's jazz recordings of Fats Waller, Duke Ellington, Count Basie, and other big bands as well as Bing Crosby, Frank Sinatra (these were Mother's favorites), and European classical music: symphonies of Beethoven and Bach and piano compositions of Chopin and Rachmaninov. My father, who studied classical piano and organ before he entered college, also had a rabid interest in politics and history.

The family's important bonding time was the weekend. Saturday afternoon chores could only be accompanied by radio broadcasts of the Metropolitan

Opera. Minnie Pearl, from the "Grand Ole Opry," serenaded us during our Saturday evening bath. On Sunday mornings we readied for church with the Negro spirituals of the Wings Over Jordan Choir. Sunday evenings were a special light supper my father prepared of delicacies that are now labeled "gourmet." We drooled over exotic cheeses, breads, and condiments from assorted ethnic groups while playing Monopoly, Chinese checkers, and Scrabble, or watching one-reel comedies of the Little Rascals or the Three Stooges on a movie projector. This was often rounded out by our singing popular classics around the piano, which both my parents and I played. My brothers played trombone and trumpet.

My mother was attentive in seeing that I learned the positive side of Blackness. At home I was encouraged to read Negro papers such as the *Pittsburgh Courier* and keep a scrapbook of black memorabilia and biographies of famous black heroes, such as Dorothy Height and Mary McLeod Bethune. I was exposed to as much black culture as possible: concerts, recitals by local artists, and a rare concert by Paul Robison, Marion Anderson, and [the] Fisk Jubilee Singers.

When it was discovered that I had dramatic talents, I recited poetry of writers such as James Weldon Johnson, Countee Cullen and Paul Laurence Dunbar at sorority or church teas, civic programs, and other social gatherings. At the age of eight, I was selected to read a Mother's Day tribute on a WHIO radio show, "The Negro Business Hour," which aired on Sunday mornings before black Daytonians left their homes for church. I was hand-somely paid and appeared several times. It was my first professional job. I also studied piano and won top prizes in citywide contests in piano and school orchestra.

The high school I attended was my first fully integrated educational experience. Knowing that an integrated high school would be an easier transition for me, my parents sent me to Roosevelt, which had the highest black population of all the Dayton high schools. I found it difficult to make friends with many black students because my way of speaking "proper" was alien to them. It was equally suspicious that I walked home after school—often with white classmates—to a neighborhood that was different from theirs. Despite the initial difficulties, I did make friends that are still in my life today.

Theodore Roosevelt High School was led by one of the most racist principals in the city. A few examples: no black girls were able to make the cheerleading squad even though our winning teams had many black players; the swim classes were separated; and there was no "official" prom, since there was a fear of girls and boys of different races mixing. However, it was known that there was a "private" dance for white juniors and seniors at the end of the school year where a king and queen were elected. We students of color knew that certain teachers' classes were to be avoided because they made sure that no black students would ever pass or make above a "D." Being black in their classes meant failing geometry, chemistry, calculus, and physics—all needed if one planned to move on to college.

Black teachers could not teach anywhere but in black high schools, though several with light complexions were able to pass. We championed them and kept their secrets. Black students were forced to have their own organizations outside of school where they could socialize and build leadership. My mother was a teen advisor to the Delta Sigma Theta interest group, Delteens. There was also a social group for girls as well as boys sponsored by Alpha Kappa Alpha sorority. This was important training for girls, in terms of culture, etiquette, self-esteem, and awareness of the part we would play in our communities as adults. When I was a junior, I was elected president of Delteens. I ran and won the Miss Negro Dayton contest; ran for Miss Jabberwock (to raise money for college scholarships); and played the organ and piano for Roosevelt assemblies and my church choirs. Just before my high school graduation, I was presented as a debutante in the Annual Debutante Cotillion—a big event in the black community.

I had assumed for my entire life that I would attend college. It was a tradition begun by my maternal grandparents who, just out of slavery, had earned college degrees. The only question was where I would go. My passions included art, fashion, and acting. I had dreams of attending an East Coast college/university or attending a design or theatre school so as to make my entry into a creative field a shoo-in. (These passions were fueled mostly by *Glamour* magazine's college issues, of which I was a devotee.) My parents believed I would come to my senses and enter a more practical field, such as teaching, once I entered a state-funded, small university that was more suited to our family income. After all, I was a Negro girl with a stable and sensible upbringing. I received three scholarships that got me in the door. I compromised by choosing a major in drama and speech at Ohio University.

I arrived with my whole family and too much luggage at my first dorm, Howard Hall. The university had chosen the living quarters as well as my roommates from Cleveland and Sandusky. It was the practice in the 1950s to place students of the same race and sex together. (When I arrived in the fall of '54, there were one hundred black students in the student body of six thousand.) There was no problem with acceptance. I could be myself. I knew I would love Ohio University.

One thing that bonded the students of color was our awareness that not every high school graduate was offered the opportunity to attend college—especially in our communities. We were the upper tenth (perhaps less), afforded much in sacrifice from our black families and communities. We were expected, by those who had sent us, to do well, keep out of trouble, and stay until we graduated with a Degree. By keeping our part of the bargain, we would be upholding not only our dreams, but also those of our families and ultimately our race. We were also the tenth that Ohio University would reject—or, tolerate if we fit into its standards.

Having arrived in Athens, we moved proudly into assigned rooms in integrated dorms, curious to know how different, or perhaps alike, we were. We had been lectured, groomed, and warned by our parents not to rock the boat and to make them prouder than they already were. That was the burden then and, thankfully to a lesser degree, fifty years later. We would either pass or fail at playing the game we had been chosen to play in a white university in racist America.

Though determined to do well academically, it was important that we have our own social network. Alpha Phi Alpha fraternity (the only black fraternal organization on campus) gave us a social calendar that helped us preserve our racial identities and an outlet that allowed us to play and relax, be ourselves, and dance to our music, forgetting how difficult it might be to keep up our grade point averages, compete with our classmates, and stop wondering for a moment if our degrees would help us have careers, even if we, as blacks, were paid less than whites.

We also congregated *en masse* in the student union after classes to forget that we missed our families and friends at home. We took over the card tables with whist tournaments and sabotaged the jukebox. When Elvis or Bill Haley and The Comets seemed to be the music of choice, we dropped our coins in favor of R & B dance music (Bill Doggett's "Night Train") and competed or danced with OU's next best dancers, who were mostly of Italian descent, in jitterbugging contests. There was less racism on those dance floors.

Incidents that I experienced that reflected the racial climate at OU between 1954 and 1958 included the chronic issue of hair. We girls hid our straightening hair combs and related paraphernalia from our white dorm mates or discreetly inquired among ourselves about whether there was a beautician nearby that "understood" our hair. Our male counterparts learned to hitch rides beyond Athens to barbershops that would cut their hair.

Perhaps more acute incidents included my first trip to the post office. A white man with his wife and two children in tow refused to allow me to walk past them on the sidewalk not far from the p. o.'s steps. The man spit at me and told me to "get off the sidewalk" because niggers were not allowed in their town. I never ventured off Court Street alone again that year.

I also found that my first professor, the director of the drama department in which I was enrolled, was cold and aloof. Finally he blatantly told me that I would never be cast in any productions because there were few or no "Negro" parts for me at Ohio University and, indeed, in legitimate theatre and that I should change to something more suitable. Nontraditional casting was beyond his imagination.

Fortunately there was a new professor from New York City in the department the next semester. His name was Tony Trisolini. I loved his passion and excitement for his craft as well as for the students. He was one of the most empathetic human beings I had ever met. He was very encouraging. He ignored the department policy of "maid-only" parts and allowed me to read for roles that would let me grow in craft and technique. When he directed his production of Shakespeare's *Macbeth*, he cast me as the first witch and designed lime-green makeup for the three witches so that we would all have the same eerie complexions and my skin color would not jar a non-accepting audience, if indeed there were one.

The same semester he further acknowledged my talent by adapting Gwendolyn Brooks' novella, *Maud Martha*, into a one-act play in which I played the lead. He vowed to groom me for the New York stage. I confided that my parents were not enthusiastic about my choice of major. He invited my mother, faculty, and student body for a special showing of the play to prove my talent, and he pleaded with my mother to allow me to remain a drama major. She was not convinced a Negro girl could ever be gainfully employed on the Broadway stage. (In 1959, a year after my graduation, an all-black cast took Broadway by storm with *A Raisin in the Sun.*) She and my father demanded that I change my major or leave school. Crestfallen and obedient, I became a speech therapy major.

Another time Tony Trisolini came to my assistance was when my godfather, who assisted me with financial aid, sent a tuition check to the university. I was called into the financial aid office and cross-examined as to why the check had not come from my parents. The director of the department accused me of having given sexual favors to acquire the money from the man taking care of my bill. When I explained that my godfather was a family friend I had known since birth, he insinuated that attractive girls such as myself were prone to that behavior. I was stunned and humiliated and left the office in tears. Professor Trisolini noticed my distress. I related what had happened. Incensed, he went to the office and came to my defense. I don't know what Tony did or said, but my parents, godfather, and I received a formal apology.

I took every elective in fields such as fine arts that suited my artistic bent. I studied the cello in the music department. Another visiting professor came from New York to teach in dance and choreography classes. In that course I choreographed a dance for a small group of dancers performing to "Voodoo Suite," an Afro-Cuban piece, along with Vachel Lindsay's poem "The Congo." She thought I should become a dance major and come to New York to pursue dance and drama. But again this fell on the deaf ears of my family. I did continue to perform and choreograph, sometimes with Hillel, a Jewish student organization, and sometimes for a fraternity's Greek Week performances.

By junior year I was hanging out with a multi-racial/cultural group of students who were the most intellectual, artistic, and edgy on campus. (One was alumnus Jim Dine, one of America's most innovative painters; another was

Adger Cowans, who has become a renowned photographer, painter, and protégé of the *Life* photographer, filmmaker, and composer Gordon Parks.) We were considered rebels and "bohemians."

One spring break (perhaps inspired by Jack Kerouac's *On the Road*), six "liberal" black and white kids spent spring break in New York, having piled into a rusting "heap" with rotting floorboards, bad brakes, and leaking oil. We were barely able to fill the gas tank and pay the Pennsylvania Turnpike tolls. Our purpose was to hang out in Greenwich Village and listen to Miles Davis, Thelonious Monk, and other famous jazz musicians and frequent the coffee houses to listen to the poetry of the Beat poets. I lied to my parents and said I would be staying with a girlfriend and would be sure to see my Aunt Helen when, in fact, I was staying in the home of a Jewish boy and his family. (This was my first large act of rebellion!) He was one of the Jewish students from Brooklyn who was part of our group. Because of a quota on Jews at New York University, he and others of his heritage were steered to the "Harvard on the Hocking." In the short time we dated, we felt the weight of being harassed and scrutinized on campus. Ohio University wrote both our parents, asking if they were aware of our interracial friendship. Both sets of parents replied that they had met and entertained both of us in their respective homes. I had "'fessed up" by that time, and my parents had no objections to our being friends. I'm sure no same-race dating couple's parents had such inquiries.

(In 1961 the parents of a white female student, Ohio University's dean of women, and President Baker were extremely perturbed when it seemed that a young woman was determined to marry a fellow student who was black.)

Our one act of protest on campus was to organize and petition to have the controversial, humanitarian folk singer, Pete Seeger and the Weavers, give a concert on campus. The House Un-American Activities Committee had declared him a communist. As a multi-racial/cultural group, we were repri-manded, threatened, ostracized, and ridiculed for our efforts. After petitioning, with assistance from liberal faculty, we finally did succeed in bringing the group to campus. These years were just prior to the civil rights movement that was stirring in this country and producing sit-ins in the South. By senior year, I think I was the first woman of color to room with a white girl at Center Dorm. Of course, we had to get permission from our parents.

The aforementioned incident took place against a backdrop of campus life that included studying in the stacks of Chubb Library, running late up and down hills to the next class, sorority and fraternity rush weeks, giving the last furtive kiss goodbye to our dates before the bell rang, and sometimes acquiring "minutes" that could total up to punishment. There were the MIA (Men's Independent Association) movies midweek, Homecoming games, occasional live music from the likes of Dave Brubeck, Paul Desmond, Count Basie, Joe Williams, The Four Freshmen, and George Shearing. Our radios tuned in Bill Doggett, The Platters, and Duke Ellington.

Eisenhower was in the White House. The selective service loomed menacingly over the male population. Korean War veterans came to campus on the GI Bill; girls were "pinned" or engaged. We endured panty raids and decorated Greek Week floats. It all seems so innocent now.

It seemed that from the time I graduated in 1958, took my first job, married, gave birth to a son and twin daughters, divorced, and survived a serious health challenge, the world had turned chaotic. It was only a span of four years, but a new horizon was emerging and there was change everywhere. I was just old enough to vote for the first time for John F. Kennedy—two days after delivering my first child. I was working my first job while black and white students were protesting and sitting in. I was envious; I wanted to help. Soon I was a single parent of three. The turbulent '60s were in full swing and I wanted to join the fray. Civil rights marches and protests were where I wanted to be. I did what I could with three babies, but one day, during a rally-turned-riot, a girlfriend and I, with our collective six children (two in strollers), found we were about to be escorted by policemen into paddy wagons for civil disobedience. That day I received a wake-up call loud and clear. I was a single parent and had responsibilities to my family. I then began rooting from the sidelines for Stokely, Malcolm, and Martin.

After the assassinations of John and Robert Kennedy, Medgar Evers, Martin Luther King Jr., Malcolm X, and the many unsung heroes, I felt cheated that I had missed out on going south to register voters. I felt I could give back to the communities these heroes gave their lives for and decided my service would be to use my skills with disadvantaged children. I headed the first Head Start speech and language project in Dayton before moving to New York in 1968 to work in a NYC Board of Education's speech and language program in Harlem.

I saw that my children and I received as many of the cultural advantages this great city offered. Our interests were music, dance, and drama. The children received training from Henry Street Settlement's great programs and eventually went to performing arts middle and high schools. I was soon able to work as an actress in Off-Broadway productions, film, television, commercials, and print modeling. This and my love for jazz eventually led to my becoming a professional singer in jazz and cabaret. In 1992 I moved to Los Angeles for ten years and worked in film, television, and stage and musical productions. I returned to New York City in 2003, where I still reside.

I write my one-woman shows and was nominated for 2007 Manhattan Association of Clubs and Cabarets best female Jazz Vocalist Award for my show *Songs in the Key of My Yesterday—Major and Minor.* I am a member of Actors' Equity Association, Screen Actors Guild, and an inactive member of Delta Sigma Theta sorority. I divide my time between work as a jazz cabaret singer and as an advocate for Housing Works, the largest organization in the world dedicated to fighting homelessness for people living with HIV/AIDS. I am especially active in advocating for women of color, the population that represents the highest number of new infections. I was part of a delegation attending the 2010 International AIDS Conference in Vienna, Austria, in July.

Adger W. Cowans, 1954–58

Adger Cowans, like Howard Nolan, seemed to have chosen his career path at an early age: he would be a photographer. Ohio University had an excellent program in photography in 1954, one of the best in the country, in fact, and so it was not surprising that Adger chose the school as his alma mater or that, given his skill, willingness to innovate, and persistence, he became the art photographer he had intended to be. His autobiographical sketch is written in the third person and presented as he submitted it.

Elva Jane Johnson and Adger Cowans were both members of Orchesis and performed in its productions. 1956 *Athena. Courtesy of the Mahn Center.*

Adger was born in 1936 in Columbus, Ohio. After graduating from high school, he enrolled in Ohio University in Athens where he studied with Clarence H. White Jr., an influential photographer whose father, Clarence H. White Sr., was a founding member of the group, Photo-Secession. According to Lee Krantz, writing in the book *American Photographers*, "Cowans' studies with Clarence H. White Jr. and Minor White were the early influences on his approach to photography as an art form."

After earning a bachelor of fine arts degree in 1958, Cowans joined the U.S. Navy, working as a navy photographer until 1960. The following year, he landed a job as an assistant to Gordon Parks at *Life* magazine. Later in his career, he would have the opportunity to work with fashion photographer, Henry Clarke, and also with Lillian Bassman and with Ben Somoroff.

During the early sixties, Cowans photographed the activities of many civil rights groups, particularly the Student Nonviolent Coordinating Committee (SNCC) and the Congress of Racial Equality (CORE). One of his most famous images is an often-reproduced portrait of Malcolm X. In 1962 he received a John Hay Whitney Foundation grant, a prestigious award that allowed him to pursue his own creative work. In 1963 he won the award for best photography at the Yolo International Exhibition in California. That same year, he launched his career as a freelance photographer.

During this time, Cowans was associated with the Boston group, the Heliographers—"heliography" being an early term for photograph—which included such notable photographers as Paul Caponigro, Jerry Uelsmann, and Eugene Smith. In 1965 Cowans had his first major exhibition at the Heliography gallery, one of the first galleries in New York to consider photography to be a "fine art" on the level with more traditional art forms, such as printing or sculpture.

Throughout the 1960s, Cowans's work was shown in exhibitions all around the world. In 1966, he exhibited his photographs at the First World Festival of Negro Arts in Dakar, Senegal. Two years later, he was included in the group shows "Photography in the Fine Arts" at the Metropolitan Museum in New York and "Photography U.S.A." at the deCordova Museum in Lincoln, Massachusetts.

In addition to his association with the Heliographers, Cowans was one of the founding members of the organization, International Black Photographers. He also belonged to the African Commune of Bad Relevant Artists (AFRICOBRA), a group that began in Chicago in the late 1960s, and the Kamoinge Workshop. He participated in several shows with members of these groups, including the Heliographers exhibition; his photographs were shown in several prestigious galleries, such as the International Center of Photography, the Chicago School of Design, and the Studio Museum in Harlem.

In the mid-1960s, Cowans began to achieve success as a still photographer for the motion picture industry. He now has more than thirty feature films to his credit, including *Cotton Comes to Harlem* (1970), *The Way We Were* (1973), *On Golden Pond* (1981), *The Cotton Club* (1984), *Dirty Dancing* (1987), and *City Hall* (1996).

In 1977 Cowans exhibited photographs at the Second World Black and African Festival of Arts and Culture in Lagos, Nigeria. Four years later, his work was included in the exhibition, "Moments" at the Greene Space Gallery in New York.

In 1994 Cowans had a mini-retrospective exhibition at the College of New Rochelle in New York, where he was an artist-in-residence. The show included more than thirty photographs—including portraits, street scenes, landscapes, and still lifes dating from the 1950s to the 1990s—as well as eighteen paintings dating from the 1970s to the 1990s. "Mr. Cowans is at his best when the subject is nature," wrote the critic Vivien Raynor in the *New York Times*. "Examples are a beautiful shot of bare trees receding, black to gray, through mist illuminated by a dim sun and the pictures of reflections in rippling water."

As for his paintings, Raynor wrote, "Mr. Cowans is craftsman enough in his prints, but in his painting he becomes obsessive. . . . With these canvases, Mr. Cowans abandons the world for a realm where there is neither humanity nor weather—only cold perfectionism expressed by means of luxuriant color and texture."

The following year, Cowans's work was shown at the Emily Lowe Gallery in Long Island, New York. "Mr. Cowans has spent many years photographing water, frozen and fluid," wrote critic Helen A. Harrison in the *New York Times*. "His pictures invite contemplation, for the nuances that emerge appear only gradually as the eye penetrates the welter of surface rhythms. Isolated from their surroundings, the images become suggestive, alluding to veiled forms that seem both tangible and ephemeral."

At the 2001 Florence Biennale of Contemporary Art, Cowans received the Lorenzo il Magnifico alla Carriera in recognition of his distinguished career. In 2007, "Running Deep," a one-man show honoring Cowans, was conducted at [Franklin &] Marshall College. In 2009 Cynthia Dantzic included him in her book, *100 New York Photographers*. Cowans's photographs have been published by such well-known periodicals as *Ebony, Esquire, Essence, Harper's Bazaar, Life, Look, Modern Photography*, the *New York Times, Paris Match, and Time*. His work has also been included in *Popular Photography*

Annual in 1966 and 1968, as well as the *Black Photographers Annual* in 1973, 1974, and 1976.

In addition to his freelance career, Cowans has taught photography classes at Wayne State University, the Cleveland Institute of Art, and the University of Michigan. His work has been collected by IBM Corporation, Rochester, New York; IMP/GEH [International Museum of Photography at George Eastman House], also in Rochester; Shado Gallery, Oregon City, Oregon; and the [Adam Clayton Powell] State Office Building in Harlem, New York.

Cowans's artistic influences are as diverse as his creative output. Among his most important influences, he lists Edward Weston, a fine-arts photographer from the early twentieth century, and Gordon Parks, a photographer for *Life* magazine. While his work might be extremely broad, Cowans brings a similar visible sensibility and perfectionism to each project. According to Vivien Raynor, he "describes himself as practicing with his eyes as a musician does with his instrument."

Carl H. Walker, 1954–56

Carl is the instigator of this book about the Soulful Bobcats; it only became a reality because of his persistence. He was one of the two men who entered Ohio University in 1954 and later began attending Soulful Reunions at his alma mater. But he was older and, in many ways, more experienced. He had been drafted, served in Korea, was wounded, and attended a Negro school in West Virginia before coming to Ohio University as a transfer student. During his two years in Athens, he fell in love with Frances Ramsey, whose biography includes him. They have made a long life together; consequently, his biography overlaps with the one Frances wrote.

I graduated from Stratton High School, Beckley, West Virginia, in 1948. My experiences there were a mixture of successes and disappointments. The successes include my playing in the high school band, singing in the glee club, developing lifelong friendships, and winning numerous regional and national awards in public speaking, parliamentary procedures, and quiz contests sponsored by the New Farmers of America (the white organization was the Future Farmers). One year, I was elected president of NFA in West Virginia, and one year I was national vice president. I won regional speaking contests at West Virginia State College and Bowie State College in Maryland. I participated in national competitions at Southern University in Louisiana, Tuskegee Institute in Alabama, and South Carolina State College. It was after returning from one of these contests that my father displayed the most affectionate and memorable time I ever spent with him. He was very proud of my successes and told me he wanted to send me to college.

My participation in the high school band and the New Farmers of America were probably the most influential and lasting experiences of my high school years.

Our vocational agriculture teacher effectively taught us self-confidence, leadership, teamwork, and the zeal to excel. He was one of the "innovative educators" Bruce Nemerov referred to in his 2009 article, "Sowing the Seeds of Leadership," where he said, "When the public education of southern blacks tried to bind them to work in the fields, innovative educators, both black and white, founded a club to teach rural students skills and cultural arts well beyond the curriculum."

On the whole, my teen years were good and enjoyable. I worked at various jobs after school almost every day. My jobs were appropriate for my age and included cleaning up at small stores, yard work, newspaper delivery, shining shoes, and washing dishes at a country club. During summer months, I had more time and played baseball with the American Legion team in addition to sandlot football and baseball.

Adult life and responsibilities were not delayed for me as my father died in December of my senior year, and one of my brothers was killed in a car accident two weeks after my high school graduation. Each had assured me that he would send me to college—but that was not to be. I immediately became responsible, along with an older sister and brother, for contributing to our family support.

Before December 1947, our immediate family was composed of my father, my mother, five boys, and two girls. I was the middle child, with girls as the oldest and youngest. My mother never worked outside the home. My father, a veteran of World War I who had served in France, worked as a coal miner for about thirty-five years. He suffered many injuries from his work, including losing all the fingers on one hand, breaking both of his arms, and being severely burned from his lower back almost to his neck. He died of silicosis (black lung disease) and a heart attack. He had a fifth-grade education; my mother completed about the sixth grade. Many of their peers considered my father a very intelligent man and relied on him to read and interpret the news. He was quite pleased with my schoolwork, especially my public-speaking contests, as he told me several times. We, like most coal mining families, did not have much money, but we had a stable and wonderful family life. My father was an extremely dedicated family man.

In retrospect, I know of several examples of my family trying to escape from the coal mines for the promise of good jobs and money in New York. The process was in motion for several years, but culminated for me in June 1948, when I moved to New York permanently. I went to work almost immediately and joined my older siblings in providing support for our mother and younger ones in West Virginia. My favorite uncle and mentor (my mother's brother) had been living in New York since his graduation from Bluefield State College in West Virginia in about 1936. I wanted to be just like him. He was a supervisory social worker and took me under his wing to learn all the things necessary for a successful life. At the time, I only knew I wanted to "work in an office." My uncle assisted me in finding a job as an office assistant (also known as office boy).

For Carl, the Korean War was a signal event of the 1950s. Certainly, it played a large part in his maturation and in his ability to afford his college education.

I was drafted into the United States Army in July 1951. I was first sent to Camp Kilmer, NJ, and then to Fort Dix, NJ, for basic infantry training. Then I sought and was assigned to the 173rd Army Band. After about three months, I was ordered overseas, to the 25th Infantry Division in Korea. I am sure I was among the first blacks in both the 25th Division Band (which contained two blacks) and the 90th Field Artillery Battalion, where there were four blacks in my gun battery.

On Mother's Day in 1952, our artillery unit experienced about a 30 percent casualty rate, including me. I was hit on my left thigh, very near my abdomen. I spent three months in hospitals in Korea and Japan and was awarded a Purple Heart. After I recovered, the army returned me to my unit and the fighting continued. During my time in Korea, I became quite aware of the importance of religion, and I also became determined to go to college on the GI Bill when I got home. Overall my military experience was quite good, and I was promoted from private to sergeant within eighteen months. When I became a sergeant, I also became the noncommissioned officer in charge of the fire-direction center for our gun battery.

When I was discharged in May 1953, I had been out of high school for five years, but I had time to apply for and gain admission to college in the fall. Two thoughts filled my mind. Which school would accept me? And do I have the ability? The first question was answered when I received an acceptance letter from West Virginia State College. The second question was clearly answered at the end of my freshman year when I won a trophy for having the highest average in the class. Actually, by the beginning of the second semester, I began to realize I could handle college work. I made plans for transferring and requested numerous college catalogs. The list narrowed to the University of Michigan, Oberlin College, and Ohio University. Ohio University was the only school I actually applied to, and I was accepted for the fall of 1954.

I arrived on campus on schedule and was assigned to Johnson Hall. My roommates were Robert Mayo and Walter Jackson, who were both from around Steubenville, Ohio. Bob graduated from OU and became an Episcopal priest, but I don't know what happened to Walter. I liked living in Johnson Hall and eating at the East Green dining hall. The feeling was similar to army life, but more luxurious. My adjustment was fairly easy because most students were friendly. The Bunch of Grapes Room at the student center facilitated social life, especially if you were black.

My love and loyalty to Ohio U began when they accepted all my credits and grades from West Virginia State College. This enabled me to complete my undergraduate work in three years because I had carried eighteen to twenty credit hours each semester at WVSC. I attended one summer session at OU. My roommate during that summer was Sylvester Davis, an Alpha Phi Alpha man from Cleveland. We became good friends. I think he went to John Carroll [University] and became a lawyer in Cleveland.

I found the academic work challenging, but not more difficult than expected. I particularly liked the history classes of Professor Volweiler and Professor Mayes.

I did encounter what I believed, then and now, to be some deep-seated racism from one of the professors in secondary education, my major field. First, in class, when I volunteered to answer questions I was usually ignored. When I was recognized and permitted to speak, my answers were rejected as incorrect. I was the only black in that class. I pointed out my dilemma to the student who sat next to me. He had a strong penchant for mischief and decided he would repeat the answers I had given and see what would happen. We found that the same answers coming from my white classmate were routinely accepted as correct.

Another indication of the professor's racist attitude was evident when I confronted him about a grade he had given me on a paper. He told me he did not like the way I wrote and that he had never found a Negro student who could write well. A few years later I found out that one of my black friends (also a Soulful Bobcat), who graduated in 1957, had been told the same thing by this professor.

For some time I wondered why black students were not "tapped" for honor societies. This question first arose when I was working on a master's degree in American civilization at the University of Maryland. Almost immediately I was inducted into Phi Alpha Theta, the national history honor society, based on the grades I had received in history courses at OU. The Maryland professors asked me why I was not admitted to the honor society while at OU. Unfortunately, I have been able to come to only one conclusion—race.

On the other hand, I also recall what seemed to me an extended experience free of racial intolerance. That was when completing my work for my BSEd. I had the opportunity to do my student teaching at the high school in The Plains under the direction of Mr. Shoemaker. It was a wonderful experience and my grade reflected mutual satisfaction with my performance.

I also believe being black had a real advantage at OU when it came to student housing in the '50s. The university wisely excluded blacks from the housing lottery and basically guaranteed us housing on campus because it was almost impossible for blacks to find housing in the town of Athens. After years of professional administrative experience, I looked back at the racial situation at OU from an administrative perspective to see whether the university was farsighted, liberal, tolerant, or bigoted. I have decided that they were probably more farsighted, making changes, but slowly. Without sufficient documentation to validate my theory, I think OU had a quota for admission of black students during the 1950s and that the quota was about one percent of the total student body. If true, this had advantages for the university: there would be relative freedom from censure for failure to accept blacks; the university could be more selective in choosing students who could be expected to graduate; the small number of acceptances made it practical to provide housing for "special" students; and a minute minority community meant the institution could more easily control volatile situations, should they arise.

The racial experience I remember most profoundly could have sparked a race riot. It occurred in the spring of my first year at OU. One evening Leon Ward, a close friend, and I went to a meeting at the black Baptist church (Mt. Zion). On the way back to campus, we walked along Court Street and decided to have a drink before returning to our dorms. Both of us were veterans and felt this was an acceptable way of closing out a busy day. We had heard that the bar on Court Street closest to the campus would serve blacks. (I think it was where Chipotle Mexican Grill is now.) We walked in, found two seats, and ordered our drinks. We were served with no question or reluctance.

After starting our drinks and continuing our conversation, a loudmouth patron began to say things like, "I haven't seen anything like this since I left Cleveland. Those boys are out of place!" He attracted a lot of attention from other patrons, who mostly encouraged him. He was a very large fellow: I would guess about 6'4" and around 275 pounds. Both Leon and I were about 5'7"; I was heaviest at 165 pounds. Leon recognized the guy because he had seen him on the East Green. The loudmouth continued to the point that we believed we would have to fight our way out of there. We only saw one door in the place. Leon reminded me in later years that we sat there and created a strategy, including throwing whiskey in his eyes and running. His rants continued throughout our one drink, but neither he nor anyone else tried to stop us or hurt us as we left. Once outside, we laughed nervously, but both of us were truly humiliated. We returned to the East Green at about 10:00 PM. We called our buddies together: Howard Nolan, Leroy Massie, Bill Henderson, Delmont Hopkins, Walter Jackson, and some others. Both Massie and Henderson were athletes and immediately recognized our description of the loudmouthed fellow. Henderson had played high school football with him in Cleveland, and Massie knew him from the OU football team. Once the identity of the loud-mouth was established, our group became more agitated.

All of us returned to the bar to adjust the wrong the loudmouth had done. In retrospect, it was truly a blessing that the fellow and his vociferous supporters had left. All of us returned to our dorms without any incident that night. However, there were strange outcomes to the experience. First, Leon Ward and I went to see the dean of men, Maurel Hunkins, the next day and reported the incident and the verbal assailant. The dean was more upset with us and blamed us for the situation. He told us it was a good thing nothing happened because, "You boys could have been kicked out of school." It appears the dean may have already known about the incident before his discussion with us.

The second outcome was that the dean summoned Howard Nolan and gave him a severe verbal reprimand for his part in the incident. A third outcome might have been the basis for the dean arranging a three-man apartment for Leon, Leroy Massie, and me for my second year. All of us were army veterans, three to five years older than our classmates. The apartment we had at 51 E. Mulberry was located under the washateria between the Episcopal church and Scott Quad. That housing was very good for us.

I was impressed with the availability of extracurricular activities offered at OU. While a student there, I played French horn in the "activities band." That group played at very informal programs and at basketball games. I was also a member of the International Club, and some of us from the East Green would get together to play softball. I escorted my girlfriend to several dances, and we often went to the movies at Mem-Aud. (The auditorium has been renamed for OU's first male and female African American graduates: Templeton Blackburn Alumni Memorial Auditorium). I remember seeing *Love Is a Many-Splendored Thing* and *The High and the Mighty* while dating Frances.

I suspect that most of my OU friends remember me mostly by my inexorable pursuit of Frances Ramsey. I never dated any other girl at OU. I graduated *cum laude* in June 1956. My mother attended my ceremony and spent some time with her future daughter-in-law. In December I went to Tuskegee to meet Frances's family and to become engaged for marriage.

After graduation I returned to New York briefly and then went to West Virginia. I was offered social work positions in WV, but I decided to move to Cleveland for higher pay and fewer racist hurdles. I would also be closer to Frances in Athens. My first position in Cleveland was as a social worker for the Cuyahoga County Department of Public Welfare. I handled family casework for welfare clients. Six months later, I was contacted by the U.S. Department of the Army, offering me a position as advisor to the Army Reserve Program. This position would give me a 50 percent increase in salary, which made my decision an easy one. After six months with the army program, I became aware of a position with the U.S. Social Security Administration. I was hired in June 1957.

I worked for the Social Security Administration for almost thirty years before retiring from the United States Government. My career with the agency was a "marriage made in heaven." It is likely that only people with intimate knowledge of the organization and its culture before the Medicare and Supplemental Security [Income] Programs in 1965 [and 1972] would understand my feeling of commitment and loyalty. The requirements for promotion in the field organization usually meant you had to go to a different city. My own route took me from Cleveland to Baltimore; to Washington DC; to Dayton, Ohio; to Detroit; to San Francisco; back to Baltimore again; and finally to Atlanta.

My civil rights activism began after our initial move to Baltimore in 1959. Baltimore was a rigidly segregated city; African Americans could not eat in white restaurants or diners or stay in many of the white hotels. I was embarrassed several times and decided to become an activist. I initially joined the NAACP (which was considered radical in Baltimore at the time) but found their approach a bit too mild for my wounded ego. I then joined the Congress of Racial Equality (CORE) and sat-in at some restaurants. SSA management did not look kindly on employee participation in public demonstrations sponsored by either organization, and I realized I could be placing my new career in jeopardy. Frances and I participated in the historic March on Washington in 1963. We also supported many activities for civil rights when we lived in DC.

As soon as we settled in Atlanta, both Frances and I continued our educational activities. In 1980 I enrolled in a PhD program at Atlanta University. After my retirement in 1986, I accepted a position there as an adjunct professor, which I continued after the school merged with Clark College. I also taught one year at Kennesaw State University near Marietta, Georgia. Following several years of classroom teaching, both undergraduate and graduate, I became a consultant for the United Negro College Fund scholarship program. I retired from all academic positions in 2007. It has been a long and enjoyable "ride" since Frances and I left Ohio University in the 1950s. Our retirements are rich with memories.

The Latecomers

During 1955, just before and shortly after the arrivals of George Ralph Hall and Alvin Clay Adams Jr. at Ohio University, several highly publicized events occurred in the Southern United States, sparking the wave of activism that came to be known as the civil rights movement.

In Mississippi, during the summer of 1955, two black men—Rev. George Lee of Belzoni and Lamar Smith of Brookhaven—were shot for standing up for African Americans' right to vote. No one was accused or apprehended. The situation was clearly appalling, but it was the murder of teenager Emmett Till on August 28 that galvanized both the national and international press and kept the horrendous story in the news for months. Till had been visiting relatives in Money, Mississippi, when he was kidnapped, shot, weighted down, and tossed into the Tallahatchie River, allegedly for whistling at a white woman. Two white men were apprehended, accused, and then, in September, acquitted by a jury of twelve white males.

On December 1, in Montgomery, Alabama, Rosa Parks, a black seamstress, refused to relinquish her seat on the bus to a white man and was arrested. That night the Women's Political Council, led by Jo Ann Robinson, called for a boycott of the city's bus system and asked twenty-six-year-old

Martin Luther King Jr. for help. The boycott lasted 381 days—until the city's white leaders capitulated.

When George Ralph Hall and Alvin Clay Adams Jr. entered Ohio University in the fall of 1955, they had definite plans for the future. George dreamed of becoming a teacher, and Alvin planned to develop his writing skills and work as a journalist. Both grew up in supportive families without their fathers. George's revered high school coach helped him with his college applications, and he received an athletic scholarship to the university. Alvin had some financial support from his family, and a high school teacher helped him get a small scholarship and a campus job.

George Ralph Hall, 1955–60

George grew up in Lincoln Heights, an all-black suburban community in Cincinnati, Ohio, where he enjoyed the healthy learning environment of his elementary school and the outdoor activities of his scout troop. He was recruited by Coach Franklin Shands to attend Saint Martin de Porres High School, a small Catholic institution for Negro boys in downtown Cincinnati. Under the "fatherly guidance" of Coach Shands, he made the honor roll all four years, participated in "all the major sports, " and learned to take advantage of every opportunity. He also continued to develop his "God-given talent" as an impressive baritone. His arrival at Ohio University was a bit of a culture shock.

I had just left an all-black environment, so it probably comes as no surprise that I was a little culture shocked when I saw only a few black students on the campus during freshman orientation. Well, much to my chagrin and utter disappointment, I discovered that there were only about nine black students living on campus and six living off campus. Fortunately by the end of my senior year in 1960, there was an estimated enrollment of about 150 black students. This number allowed several black sorority and fraternity organizations to coexist on campus, despite the university's position that minorities couldn't support four black organizations.

Alvin Eugene Wesley (*front row, fourth from left*) and George R. Hall (*back row, sixth from left*) were residents of Tiffin Hall. 1957 *Athena. Courtesy of the Mahn Center.*

Ohio University slowly became my home away from home. I continued to play basketball both my freshman and sophomore years. I played the guard position because the center position was given to a taller teammate who stood 6'8" to my 6'4". The Bobcats competed aggressively with all the schools in the Mid-American Conference, which consisted of Bowling Green, Miami, Kent State, Akron, Buffalo [NY], Ball State and all [other] Ohio schools. Historically, we weren't too much favored by the MAC to compete in the first round, quarterfinals, semifinals, or finals in basketball.

My scholarship required me to run track all four years in the high/low hurdles and 440 meter relay race. We won the MAC meets two of the four years I competed. I can truthfully say that I competed with the best, though personally I was never a frontrunner. I saw a lot of backsides of well-known hurdlers during the 1957–59 seasons! I did, however, hold the record in the 400 meter high hurdles in 1958, with a time of 56 seconds. This sport took me on extensive road trips to Michigan, although most track meets were held in Ohio.

Not all the road trips were exciting or fun because we were hit with racism on occasion. I remember leaving Maysville, Kentucky, heading back to OU and the team bus stopping to have dinner. The track team was about

95 percent white. Once we were seated, the waitress took everyone's order except the black runners'. It took a second to realize what she had done. But when it hit all of us, Coach Stan [Huntsman] instructed everybody to get up and leave, including the white runners! We felt terrible that we were the cause of no one eating (as hungry and tired as we all were); however, we felt very proud to have our coach and fellow teammates take a stand like that. The white boys even urinated in protest outside the restaurant and made sure the waitress saw them do it.

There were Saturday classes, but members of the track and basketball teams missed them when we were out of town for weekend meets and games. Some professors weren't too fond of this and gave exams and pop quizzes to quietly protest. Consequently, my GPA began to suffer and slumped to 1.5, which was grounds for academic probation. This meant I was in jeopardy of losing my scholarship if I didn't raise my GPA to a 2.0 by the end of the semester. My counselor, Dr. Schuler, explained that if that happened, I couldn't return to school unless I was prepared to pay out-of-pocket for my tuition. I had come too far and sacrificed too much to squander what my athletic and academic prowess had given me! So I made some immediate and serious adjustments in my study habits and ended the school year with an overall 2.7. Whew, that was close.

Things leveled out a bit as my sophomore year rolled around, which is when I decided my major of elementary education with a minor in physical education. My studies became the main focus for the last three years of college. I applied for a dormitory counselor's job at Tiffin and got it. Working gave me a chance to save more money and have some sort of life. Every penny helped. Luckily, my weekly entertainment budget of $5.00 gave me the luxury of taking a date to the campus movie night on Wednesdays, plus buy a snack and two cokes. Most black students gathered at the student center for recreation and social activities. Places for us to party were pretty much limited to the center, so we gave the Bunch of Grapes Room some flavor. In our unique, fun-loving, and sometimes loud way, we got our party on, much to the dismay of our fellow white students.

I remember the NAACP having to intervene and serve a public violation notice to OU after the campus newspaper published a photo of black students dancing in the Bunch of Grapes Room with the caption reading, "the Bunch of Apes Room." Needless to say, this caused more racial tension than what was already prevailing across the campus. This type of racial situation was occasionally challenged by some campus organizations and the one black church in town. The '50s through the '60s were critical years of segregation and racial discrimination in the United States. Ohio University was no exception. The denunciation of black students playing certain sports, like swimming and baseball, was ever increasing and met with hostile protests.

The university had hesitantly accepted one black fraternity on campus. The threat of a second one was met with some resistance by the administration. The impetus for a second group came from eighteen young black pledges (including myself), who were subjected to hazing by members of Alpha Phi Alpha. Late on a Saturday night, we were driven thirteen miles outside the town of Nelsonville, Ohio. Our shoes were taken and we were made to walk back to campus. We arrived back early Monday morning and still made our classes. Fuming mad, we withdrew our pledges and formed an interest group in the Kappa Alpha Psi fraternity. We had to drive about four hours to Wilberforce University in Xenia, Ohio, to begin initiation and orientation. After six months of commuting, our eighteen courageous souls became the official chapter of the Kappa Alpha Psi fraternity to share the campus with the Alpha Phi Alphas of Ohio University.

My plate was full, so there was no real time for the ladies. Although I did date, I had no serious relationships in college. As a freshman I had observed several student athletes struggle with their grades and athletic performance due to too much romancing the stone, so to speak—an obsession with the ladies for sure. Lots of social activities did have negative effects on their grades, especially as freshmen trying to adjust to college life. Much of my time, I'd say about 95 percent, was consumed with schoolwork, work, sports, and frat-boy, player-type things. I spent my summers going home to work at Philip Carey, Proctor & Gamble, and the Howard Johnson Restaurant. Packed in the "Blue Goose," my friends and I rode out faithfully. In exchange for a ride home, I would charge them gas money, which was about 22 cents per gallon.

The "Blue Goose" was my beloved first car and was ideal for an unattached, tall, dark, and handsome frat boy. I bought it the summer after my freshman year. I actually worked and managed to save enough for a down payment on the four-door beauty. My mother had co-signed because I had no established credit; in fact, she made the monthly payments when I returned to school. The "Blue Goose" was slate blue and rode as smooth as velvet. With the help of my frat brothers, it was kept in tip-top shape. They always had to go somewhere, so I ran a small operation that kept a little money in my pocket. Trips to nearby Columbus, Cleveland, Dayton—you name it—the "Blue Goose" got us there. There was no barbershop in Athens that would serve black patrons, so six of my frat brothers and I would gas up the Goose and cruise to Parkersburg, West Virginia. We didn't mind; it was a monthly treat, plus our way to stay fresh and clean for the ladies. Enough said!

I accepted my required teaching student teaching assignment at the Putnam Lab Elementary School [Ohio University Elementary School in Putnam Hall] in September 1959. Putnam was where OU professors' children attended school. The fifth-grade teacher, Mr. Shrigley, informed me that I was the first black male student teacher. I didn't know whether to feel intimidated, honored, or both. But my experience was a wonderful and challenging one. All eyes were on me, seemingly. The class of twenty white fifth-grade students was sort of mesmerized by my 6'4" stature and commanding voice. Thinking back, I can honestly say that my first student teaching experience was a delightful one, filled with tremendous parental support, unparalleled respect at such a young age, and generous cooperation from the students.

The procedure was to observe the lead teacher, Mr. Shrigley, for a few days, then assist him for another few days, progress to working with a small group, and then finally take over the entire class. Much to my surprise, after only three days of observation, Mr. Shrigley decided to forego normal procedures by having me take over the class. Was I surprised? Yes! Was I ready to take over? You betcha!

Mr. Shrigley announced to the class that I would be the teacher for the next six weeks and had full responsibility for the classroom—facilitating all five subjects, student problems, grades, and parent conferences. Following this speech, Mr. Shrigley left the classroom. It was now me against the world, at least I thought so that day. The moment had finally come for me to teach as I had dreamed of since sixth grade.

The only challenge that required me to exert my authority came when a student named John stood up in class, said nothing, but refused to sit down despite several commands to do so. He was not being disruptive. The students were used to it. Mr. Shrigley had informed me that he would allow John to stand until he was ready to sit down. Well, my patience grew very thin, and I began walking toward John, telling him to take his seat in a very commanding tone. When I got within reaching distance, John sat down quietly and class activities resumed in normal fashion. Regardless of his behavioral problems, I knew that, whatever the outcome, I had to help him save face in front of his peers and not make him uncomfortable or trapped. When he finally sat down, I smiled at him approvingly and thanked him for cooperating. This was not my standard of acceptable behavior, so I chose to find a solution that would be acceptable to me as the teacher and to little John. From that moment on and for the remaining six weeks, John became a model student and never stood up again.

I completed my six weeks of student teaching in December of 1959, right before Christmas. After spending the holiday break at home in Lincoln Heights, I returned to graduate in a formal cap-and-gown ceremony. My whole family was with me. I know they were all very proud. I recognized at that moment, more than ever, that I had always been called to teach.

Right before graduation I received a letter from the army draft board stating that I'd be drafted shortly after getting my degree in January 1960. I had participated in OU's Air Force Reserve Officer training class for two years but chose to get out my senior year because of my desire to teach. So in February 1960, I applied for an elementary teaching position in the Cincinnati Public School System and joined the Army Reserve (USAR) for six months of active duty. I was stationed at Fort Knox, Kentucky, until July. Fortunately, I was hired to teach at William Howard Taft Elementary School in Cincinnati on August 12, 1960. The feeling of accomplishment and excitement were beyond words!

I was one of four minority teachers hired to help integrate Taft, which was 60 percent black and 40 percent white Appalachians. In addition to teaching my classes, I was given many opportunities to demonstrate my leadership skills. My students were respectful and cooperative. Their parents believed in me and were extremely supportive. While there, I worked in the evenings and on weekends to complete a master's degree in elementary school administration and guidance counseling at Xavier University. I graduated in 1968.

Soon after, I was promoted to the McMillan Rehabilitation Center as an administrator and teacher in charge of high school dropouts. The Center's objective was to assist these students in completing their graduation requirements by earning General Education Development degrees (GEDs). That summer I spent six weeks as principal at Douglas Elementary School, overseeing an enrichment program.

Shortly after, I was appointed assistant principal at Madisonville Elementary, where I spent two years before applying for the position of principal at Princeton Junior High. The Princeton School System and Lincoln Heights System were consolidated in early 1970 by order of the Ohio Department of Education. The merger resulted in a complete desegregation of all staff, certified and classified. Newly hired African American teachers and administrators were assigned to positions throughout the district. I was hired to find and recruit administrators from outside the Princeton City School District.

If we recall the three decades of school desegregation, beginning with *Brown v. Board of Education* in 1954, then the merger of the two school systems was not by accident. The "Princeton Plan" was part of the strategy of mixing races in order to address disparities in the education of African American children, other minorities, and others living in poverty. I later learned that the merger was not a benevolent gesture by the Princeton School Board, but an unwanted merger that the Princeton community resisted until the citizens of Lincoln Heights threatened a lawsuit.

During my year at Princeton, I was in charge of discipline. When I found that most teachers had paddles and other "weapons" in their classrooms and that minority students were the most frequent victims of punishment, I outlawed paddling at the eighth grade and found more constructive ways to handle discipline problems. The following year, 1970, I landed at the Glendale Elementary School as its first African American principal. Glendale was the community where slaves had come on the Underground Railroad as they escaped north to freedom more than a century earlier. The school population was approximately 500 in grades K–5. About 60 percent were white and

40 percent were black. Most of the black students were bused from Hollydale, a black community.

During my first month there, my secretary brought me an antiquated folder. Astonishingly, it was my actual cumulative school record from kindergarten at a school only two blocks away. As I read, I came across the negative comments that my teacher had made about me: "George has no initiative and no doubt won't become much of anything." As I reminisced about my days under her hand, I vowed to make every student interaction a positive one and to ensure that my staff did the same. No child in my care was ever going to carry the disturbing emotional, mental, and psychological baggage I had. No, not even one!

After eleven years at Glendale and one year as the Princeton District's administrative assistant of state and federal programs, my career path led me to Cleveland, Ohio. In 1983 I became principal of Randallwood Middle School. I left there to become principal in another suburban district, Maple Heights, which was being challenged by the NAACP for not hiring African American administrators. After an interview, for which I had prepared carefully, I was offered the job of principal of Stafford Heights Elementary School.

I soon discovered that most of the teachers at Stafford Heights had been reassigned there because they hadn't worked out at other schools. The district had also gone through a "white" transition over the past five years. I wondered if the superintendent had set me up for failure, especially when it was clear that members of the PTA felt empowered to try to run the school. Fortunately, I had the support of many parents, and by the end of the year I had restored the school's positive image.

When problems with the superintendent intensified during my second year, I took two actions: I filed an EEOC civil complaint against him for disparate and discriminatory treatment, and I checked on my retirement status with the State Teachers Retirement System in Columbus. I found I had thirty-one years in service and that, by working until February of 1990, I could easily retire. My decision was clear—it was time to retire, relocate, and change careers. Shortly, I found myself in Florida with a new attitude.

While in Jacksonville for Thanksgiving in 1989, I interviewed for a part-time position and ended up with a full-time offer as human resources staffing supervisor effective February 1990. Funny how things work! I happily turned in my resignation and paperwork, attended a farewell party, and was on my merry way to Florida. I was there for two years before relocating to Marietta, Georgia, to serve as assistant principal at Marietta Middle School. After two years there and a few years in different positions around Georgia, I retired for the second time.

Since my days at Ohio University, my journey has been about overcoming obstacles, pursuing dreams, and inspiring others to be productive citizens of society. My watchword is "Remember, every moment is a teachable moment."

Alvin Clay Adams Jr., 1955–59

Alvin enrolled in Ohio University's Journalism School in 1955. He was born in Morgan County, just beyond the Athens County line, grew up in the Athens area, and became the first African American to graduate from Ohio University with a degree from the School of Journalism. Like another graduate of the university, photographer Adger Cowans, he soon found himself covering the increasingly violent events of the civil rights movement. On October 19, 2007, almost fifty years after Alvin graduated and began his career, Ohio University dedicated its newest building, Adams Hall, in his honor. Alvin did not live to attend the dedication at which his alma mater ensured he would be remembered. But his life is recalled by his wife, Ada Woodson Adams, Ohio University, '61, and their children, Dr. Amelia Marie Adams and A. Clay Adams, III, in "Reflections on 'What you are is where you were when,'" which they wrote.

Ada Adams: Who was this man? What did he do? Why him in naming a major building at Ohio University? I knew Alvin was a special, loving, and caring man, but I am his wife. I had no idea that others thought of him as a person whom they loved and admired, as important enough to name the newest residence hall after him. This news came as a complete, pleasing, and overwhelming shock to me and to his family.

Reflecting on his life and our life together and sharing those reflections may give you a picture of the experiences that gave others an understanding of the man and how one's life can make a difference and an impact on others.

Dr. Maria Adams: Having spent a good portion of my life as a member of the academic environment, I've always wondered about buildings and how decisions are made regarding their names. There is always the portrait and the plaque, and this leads me to wonder abut the person and who they were and what they had done to receive such an honor. And now, in this very surreal moment, I really do know this person and who he was and what he was about. But I think into the future, years from now, when he will be the guy in the portrait whom they named the building after, and people may not remember exactly who he was and what he was about. My brother and I would like to share some things about our father to help you understand why his name is on this building.

My father began his life—as he liked to tell it—in a coal-mining shack at the foot of Carr Hill, which is in Morgan County, Ohio, just a step across the Athens County line. My brother Clay will tell you more about my Dad's beginnings and early history. For now, understand that he started life in a poor, rural, large extended family. He was a shy, reserved child who liked words far more than he liked farming and mining.

A. Clay Adams, III: My father wrote a book in 1983 called *Hold Tight to the Hames.* The book starts out with a quote from sociologist Dr. Morris Massey: "What you are is where you were when." What you are is where you were when. No quote could better summarize my father.

His family had good times and bad times, bad times that most of us couldn't even imagine nowadays; but through it all he grew up to be an intelligent, respectful, and decent young man who even went on to become the first black graduate of Ohio University's School of Journalism.

Alvin C. Adams Jr. was born a poor colored ("colored" was the term used at the time) boy just down the road from here. He never knew his father; he died in 1938. He was raised by his mother, his sister Dessie, and himself— sometimes living with other relatives in a house bristling with his uncles, and aunts, and grandparents. There weren't always opportunities for people of color where he was born, and his family would move wherever they had to to find those opportunities. Sometimes that meant a third floor walk-up in Columbus, Ohio, and sometimes it meant his grandparents' house in the rolling hills and gentle valleys that surround the city of Athens.

He didn't let these things discourage him; instead, he used them as a source of strength. Buildings are usually named after someone who gives a lot of money, but that is not true in his case. He didn't live or die a rich man, but because of the greatness of his heart, the kindness of his words, and the generosity of his spirit, he lived and died as the wealthiest man I have ever known.

My father would say, "What you are is where you were when." How did this poor, colored kid get to OU? How did his mother, making less than five dollars a day doing housework and raising two children and four younger brothers and sisters, find a way to send him to college?

It was understood by the family that Alvin needed to attend college. This goal became a reality through the help of all his family, who loved, supported, and sacrificed for him, and through the help of people like Mrs. Bonnie Kendall, his Coolville High School teacher. She saw in him a gifted writer. She knew Al's family's financial situation and knew there was not money for college but, somewhere along the line, it was decided that Alvin would go to college.

Bonnie Kendall took Alvin to Ohio University and introduced him to L. J. Hortin, head of Ohio University's School of Journalism. She told him that Alvin would soon be entering the journalism school and asked Mr. Hortin to look out for him. Ada Adams remembers that between a $100 scholarship, $100 that Alvin and the family had saved, and a sixteen-hour-a-week job as a janitor, Alvin became an OU student in 1955. He could not afford to live in campus housing and commuted to school.

The head janitor at Chubb Library, the main library at the time, befriended Alvin and allowed him to have a room—a closet underneath the staircase in the janitorial area of Chubb. Alvin caught a ride with his mother or others as they went to their housekeeping day jobs in Athens. Having the room gave him a place to do his class work, study, and rest during the day.

Dr. Hortin did look out for Alvin. Getting good grades was difficult for black students at this time. A black student had to work extremely hard to achieve academic success. Alvin experienced this in his major as his work was scrutinized and given less merit than deserved. Dr. Hortin told Alvin that his chosen field was a white man's occupation and that it was going to be difficult for him to break barriers and find work in the field. While his white journalism classmates had jobs lined up before graduation, Alvin was turned down for every position he applied for. He took a construction job.

Ada Adams: Alvin and I had met at the roller-skating rink in Nelsonville the spring before I entered Ohio University in 1957. After my first year on campus, I could no longer afford university housing and, needing a place to hang out during the day, the library stacks became that place for me.

Blacks did not feel as connected to the university as white students did because they were excluded from the mainstream of campus life. Historically, at this time, it was the practice to isolate blacks from campus activities. Looking through the *Athena*, the OU yearbooks, from 1956–59, the black presence is not prominently seen. Even in 1959, when Phillip Saunders became not only the first African American to be elected senior class president, but the first to be chosen drum major of the university band, the events did not generate much attention. As drum major he is shown in the yearbook seated cross-legged on the floor rather than marching in full stride ahead of the drums and brass. Phil went on to become a great artist, playwright, and radio personality in Chicago. Blacks on campus had so many talents that went untapped and unrecognized just because of the color of their skin.

We found places we could congregate and socialize, such as the local Baptist church, Baker Center's Bunch of Grapes Room, and off-campus locations like skating rinks and state parks. We connected here—if not to the university—at least as a unit striving to gain an education in a semihostile environment. To fulfill my teaching requirement, I had to go to Cleveland to do my student teaching. None of the schools in the surrounding area would accept us because of the color of our skin.

Efforts made while trying to connect to the university included forming our own organizations. Alvin was part of the founding group that brought Kappa Alpha Psi, a national fraternity, to campus, albeit as a social club called Kappa Phi Psi. OU denied the national group the opportunity to become an official fraternity because one black fraternity (APA) was considered enough. So, Al and his brothers went off campus to be recognized and brought the Kappas on campus in 1957. But the group was not recognized until '59, and then only as a social club.

The university did give us a good education and a foundation to build on, and we had the courage, the tenacity, and strength not to give up or quit in the face of denials. After one summer of construction work, Alvin landed a job as a reporter with the *Chicago Defender*. He met and interviewed Billy Graham. He related that once at a dinner with Graham everyone had to quote a verse from the Bible. Being almost the last of the group to speak, Alvin realized that all those verses he could remember had already been said. But somehow, after an embarrassing silence, he was able to say a verse.

Another encounter was with President Harry Truman. A comment Truman had made was disparaging to blacks. Al ran the story, and it caused quite a stir. Alvin also was introduced to real prejudice toward blacks when he worked for Johnson Publishing Company's *Jet* magazine. His assignment was to cover the civil rights movement. There were the Bull Conners and the George Wallaces of Alabama as well as those connected to the Ku Klux Klan who did not care if the black man was a reporter of a well-known national news organization. If he got in their way, or they thought he was causing trouble, he could be hosed with high-power water, attacked by dogs, or killed.

Alvin covered the civil rights movement from 1961–66 for *Jet*. During that time, he interviewed and worked with both leaders and foot soldiers, including Martin Luther King Jr., Elijah Mohammed, Malcolm X, Mohammed Ali, Fred Shuttlesworth, John Lewis, Andrew Young, Fanny Lou Hamer, Bob Moses, Mary Lane, and many others. He wanted me to experience what he had been reporting. So we took leave from our jobs and joined the movement. During this time, I had a chance to fully understand the injustices and atrocities those in the movement had to face, as well as the commitment of those who lived their daily lives facing the danger of lost jobs and of death by standing up for their right to vote and be counted as American citizens.

The old, the young, the Mary Lanes, and the Fannie Lou Hamers were our mentors and inspiration. The Green family, who opened their home to us, had come face to face with death. The bedroom where their family slept had bullet holes in the wall where one night bullets flew just inches over their bed. I looked at those holes as we too slept in that room—only imagining the fear and praying that no bullets would come again. They were shot at; crosses were burned in front of their homes or churches. They were jailed and risked their lives helping others register so they could vote.

After leaving Chicago, Alvin had a long career in public relations working for the United Auto Workers, the state of Illinois, and the Illinois Power Company. He and Ada owned, and Ada operated, the Oakland Market and Deli in Decatur, Illinois, which was recognized as an Outstanding Business by Millikin University Tabor School of Business. Senator Everett Dirkson recognized the market and the Adamses in the United States Congressional Record.

Alvin co-founded two genealogy groups: the African-American Cultural & Genealogical Society of Illinois in Decatur and, after retirement, with Ada, the Multicultural Genealogical Center in Chesterhill, Morgan County, Ohio. Through this second organization, they helped promote an understanding of individual histories in southeast Ohio and, with the help of OU's African American Studies Department, initiated Community and Campus Day in 2002 to unite the local community and Ohio University. The event showcases community talents and history and OU's diverse opportunities.

After Alvin's death, Ada continues the work of the Multicultural Genealogical Center and fosters connections with the university. During the school's bicentennial, Ada and Nancy Aiken wrote *A Significant Presence: A Pictorial Glimpse of the Black Experience in Athens County, Ohio*, to celebrate, honor, and showcase the contributions of African Americans to the university and the county.

Alvin wrote this foreword to his book *Hold Tight to the Hames*:

In the early 1980s, I was twenty-three years, six professional jobs, and two states removed from the memories of my youth. The yearning to recall and record an incident of those days in southeastern Ohio led to a collection of anecdotes that became a book. Revisiting the scenes of the events to gather facts and refresh my memory required more than our usual one or two trips a year "home" from Illinois. And these frequent trips intensified my anticipation of the eventual return to my native land. The opportunity to live again in southeast Ohio was still fifteen years in the future. But the acquaintances rekindled, with the people, places, and things of a bygone era of my existence, were a siren song, luring me undeniably back to where I belonged.

I stumbled into the ungrammatical but alliterative title for this collection while searching the dictionary for help on another project. Fate paused my fingers on a page with the illustration and definition of "hame: One of two curved projections which are attached to the collar of a draft horse and to which the traces are fastened." Instantly I recognized the value of this discovery as a title. Yet, I lingered, studying the word again and again. Something about it didn't ring true. Then it hit me. *We did not call this piece of the harness equipment "hames"; it was "haines."*

Twenty-three years of experiences away from the hills of home had taught me that words, phrases, and concepts of my youth often were askance from "dictionary English" and "proper" ideas. Even my dialect had always been out of place no matter where we had moved—so distinctive that seldom when I called a news source the second time did I have to identify myself by name.

Realizing this had presented me the first intellectual, and perhaps moral dilemma since graduation from college. Should my speech and other habits reflect the lifestyle to which I aspired, or should they hold true to my heritage? *Hold Tight to the Hames* symbolizes the choice I made. Literate enough to know that the proper adverb is "tightly," but astute enough as a writer and editor to recognize what an awful title that word would make, I opted for the eye-catching phrase.

Similarly, in one of the stories I talk about gravy made with water instead of milk. Thus, in the vernacular of my culture, "water gravy." I chuckled when a local newsman—one under whom I'd served both news writing and editing internships—wrote about my story of "watery gravy." We each defined the phrase by our respective upbringings and neither saw a need to use the other's "learning."

For the most part, our need today to hold tight to the hames is figurative rather than literal, as it once was for me, with the hames representing my memories and our values. Being able to retain the values of one's heritage, even when out-of-step with mainstream culture, is what *Hold Tight to the Hames* is all about. After all, it is the values of one's life, more than polish, that matter.

Incidentally, when the book arrived at my home, fresh off the presses of an Illinois printer in 1983, I was delighted to see stenciled on each

box—evidently by a local "farm boy" now working in the printing industry
—the title, Hold Tight to the Haines.

At the dedication of Adams Hall, President Roderick McDavis said of Alvin
Adams, "He left a wonderful legacy—a legacy of which we are very proud and
which we will always remember." Alvin's son added, "My father never forgot
that 'where you are is where you were when.' My father's belief that this
institution, Ohio University, gave him a chance at a life that was simply unthink-
able at the time he was enrolled here—that Ohio University could still be the
best chance for so many young people, even today, to better themselves, to lift
themselves up and, in doing so, to lift up the generations that come after them,
that will come after us all, was so strong that he spent some of his last days
doing whatever he could to support his alma mater."

(This biographical sketch comments on Alvin's efforts to establish a
second black fraternity on campus. Though there is no evidence from the
Minutes of the Board of Trustees that the administration actively opposed
this effort, there is evidence of concern [in minutes from 1955] that blacks
were excluded from white Greek organizations because of "restrictive
clauses in their charters." According to a 1964 study by the League of Women
Voters of Athens, by 1961 all sororities and fraternities had to remove any
exclusion statements from their charters. Also worth noting is that two
years after the establishment of Kappa Alpha Alpha sorority, *Ebony* magazine published an article praising the group "as a shining example of the
integration of a white girl into a Negro group. . . . Two years ago, when
Mary Anne Patterson joined a [KAA] sorority, there were some lifted eye-
brows. Today, she is pledge mistress of the group and one of its most popular
members." [There is no evidence that any white sorority at Ohio University had, by this time, pledged a black member.])
During the four years that the last two Negro students who would become Soulful Bobcats were at Ohio University, the push for integration
continued. In 1956, the first African American student, Autherine Lucy,
was admitted to the University of Alabama, and the U.S. Supreme Court
upheld a ruling that Montgomery's segregated bus system was unconstitu-

Lois McGuire was runner-up for Queen
of the Military Ball. 1959 *Athena.*
Courtesy of the Mahn Center.

tional. In 1957, President Eisenhower
sent federal troops to Little Rock,
Arkansas, to protect students who
were trying to integrate Central High
School, and a civil rights bill established the U.S. Commission on Civil
Rights and the U.S. Department
of Justice Civil Rights Division.
On February 1, 1960, four students
staged a sit-in at a segregated Wool-
worth's lunch counter in Greens-
boro, North Carolina.

Lois Thompson Green and Paul
Gates were undoubtedly aware of these events. Lois was, like Alvin Adams,
a "local," who grew up in The Plains. In fact, she was the daughter of Mr.
Thompson, the barber who cut so many heads of hair of the university's
male students in the '50s. She became the dear friend of Les Carney and
many other patrons of her father as well as of her university classmates.
Paul, from Middletown in southwestern Ohio, attended an integrated
high school and, by the time he entered Ohio University, was an experienced competitor in oratorical declamation and a winning athlete on the
tennis court. He continued to pursue both activities at the university. Like
many 1950s graduates of Ohio University, his career was in education.

Lois Thompson Green, 1956–60

My recollections of the "Good Ol' Days" in Athens and as a student at Ohio
University is somewhat unique, to say the least. I was born Lois Thompson
(nicknamed "Wicki" by a younger brother) and reared at The Plains, Ohio,

approximately three miles from Athens and the university. However, from birth my life was intertwined with the university and the community, and some would refer to me as a "Townie" or a "local."

My parents, Herbert and Emma Thompson, moved to Athens shortly after their marriage. After nearly sixteen years, they had their first child, Herbert Thompson Jr. Later, a son, Lloyd, and a daughter, Gracie, were born. Herb and Emma purchased a small house with several acres of land, where they moved with the three children. Herb added several rooms to the house to accommodate their three additional children, Charles, Lois, and Carlos. They thought of having a dozen children but decided a half-dozen would do, given the issues they confronted as the only African American family in The Plains school system. (The Thompsons were the first African American family to send all six of their children through twelve years of school there.)

Herbert, known as Herb in the community, worked as a coal miner, carpenter, farmer, automobile mechanic, and barber over a period of years to support his family. After Gracie enrolled at Ohio University and graduated in 1957 and Lois enrolled in 1956, Emma took a job at OU as a seamstress, making aprons and jackets for employees and students who worked in the school's cafeterias. She had worked in wealthy family homes as a seamstress for many years prior to her position at OU.

Because my family was one of a few "colored," "Negro," "black" or "African American" families (depending on what era you are talking about) who lived in the community, I saw Ohio University and Athens from a different point of view than most students who came from Columbus, Dayton, Cleveland, Cincinnati, Toledo, and other large cities. I was always amused when they complained about the hills. I was so accustomed to the hills that I did not notice they were more than a bump in the road that caused our muffler to fall off the car when spring thaws came. Also, because I lived on a hill in The Plains, I did not realize the number of hours, days, and weeks the students spent chasing their clothes, books, furniture, and cars during the frequent flooding of the Hocking River.

Many services for black students at Ohio University were limited or non-existent up until the 1950s. One area, recognized by President Baker, was the growing need for a barber for African American students. He drove to our house in The Plains and asked my dad to fill that role and Dad agreed. Although he had no formal barber schooling, he was very experienced and meticulous and had practiced for many years. He operated a small one-chair shop in the basement of our home.

Many Saturday nights, our living room was filled with students joking, laughing, and roasting one another while they waited their turn to get a haircut. Since there were only one or two cars among the guys on campus, they came in packs. My mom would provide snacks. What fun and excitement for me, as a high school student, to check out the cute guys from college. Of course, Dad was secluded in the basement, cutting hair, and had no clue what I was doing. Good for me! These were the highlight of my high school years, especially since there were no blacks around during the weekdays except my brothers and my sister. To some of the guys I became a sort of little sister away from home; to others I was someone they might date after I graduated high school and enrolled at OU.

Beside a couple of sites in Athens and the K of C Hall near campus, our house was often a place where students would gather for food, horseback riding, ball games, and just plain old family fun. To many it was a home away from home. Let me not omit the fun-filled gatherings at the Baker Center in the Bunch of Grapes Room. Words cannot express how the good times did roll. The hamburgers, french fries, dancing, laughing, and making new friends could not be replaced with anything better.

Walking across the footbridge to the football games in herds was the quickest way to get to the Bobcat stadium, to get the best seats, to be noticed by the football players we had crushes on. Saturdays could not have been more exciting as we screamed and cheered our Bobcats on to victory (or not) while stuffing our faces with hotdogs and pop.

I am sure you all remember the Mt. Zion Baptist Church. Going to church was as much a requirement as taking a bath every night. If my mom couldn't go, which was rare, she sent the kids with neighbors; no headaches, toothaches, or skinned-up knees were allowed as excuses for missing Sunday school and church. I remember the older sister Pettiford who played hymns on the pipe organ while the pews were packed with OU students, singing at the top of their lungs, sleeping, eating snacks out of their purses, gazing out the beautiful stained glass windows, or fanning furiously during hot weather since no air conditioning was available. We all loved being in church with our friends and classmates. You could hear some of us letting out a few giggles when the preacher talked about a "don't do" subject we knew we were guilty of participating in. The snacks in the basement were homemade by the older sisters, and we sure chowed them down. Best sandwiches and cookies you ever ate. Now those were the good ol' days.

Those memories still linger after fifty years. This was evident at the 2010 Soulful Alumni Reunion as we shared stories, pictures, and laughs. My Ohio University/Athens, Ohio, experiences had a tremendous influence on my life and caused me to be extremely thankful for my education, friendships, and memories. In many cases they have served as steppingstones to accomplishments for my son, daughter, four granddaughters, and twin grandsons.

Paul Gates, 1956–60

I was born in Middletown in southwestern Ohio. I am the third eldest of eleven children. I attended Middletown Public Schools, graduating in 1956. My high school was integrated, and blacks, at that time, experienced racism; however, I did not let that prevent me from participating in the activities of the school. I was a member of, or participated in, Buckeye Boys' State, Citizens' Club, Hi-Y, intramurals, Junior Classical League, Junior Homeroom Representative, Junior Literary Club, Marching Band, National Forensic League, National Honor Society, National Thespians, Prom Committee, Student Council, tennis team, and yearbook staff.

My involvement in National Forensic League provided me the opportunity to travel around the state, participating in speech tournaments. My category was oratorical declamation. During my senior year, I won several of the prep tournaments for state competition. I won first in the district tournament, which qualified me for the regional competition held at Ohio University in the spring of 1956. I was first in the regional competition, which qualified me for the state finals held at Ohio State University. I placed fourth there.

I also enjoyed the tennis team. It also allowed me to travel extensively and to meet many different people. During my senior year, my doubles partner and

I won our league championship and the Dayton District Championship, which qualified us for the finals at OSU. We placed third overall in the state.

In the fall of 1956, I started at Ohio University. It was the result of my experience there at the regional speech tournament the previous spring. I had been given a tour of the university and had the chance to speak to several students who really talked up the school. There was not a great opportunity for blacks to receive scholarships, although I did manage one from the Eastern Stars as well as an athletic scholarship to play tennis at OU. At that time, the athletic scholarship consisted of a board job. The athlete had to work, usually in one of the dining halls, for two-and-a-half hours a day, unless his sport was in season. Then he would only have to work one hour a day.

Racism existed at Ohio University, but it was no more than the racism I experienced in regular society at the time. The closest thing to overt racism at Ohio was my botany professor during my freshman year. This professor was from North Carolina and told me he did not think I could earn more than a "C" in his class. That was when I had challenged him about a grade I received on a test.

My experiences at Ohio University were quite memorable, and I took an active part in as many activities as possible, including Alpha Phi Alpha (president my senior year), Eta Sigma Phi (Classical Language Honorary), Omicron Delta Kappa (National Men's Leadership Honorary), Marching Band (drum major for two years), Orchesis (dance ensemble), intramurals, varsity tennis and track teams, Varsity O Club, and East Green Council (secretary my sophomore year).

Who can ever forget dashing across the campus with a date in order for her to reach her dorm before 10:00 PM during the week and midnight on the weekends and avoid acquiring "minutes" that could lead to being campused for a week. Standing in line to cross the footbridge to get to the football stadium could sometimes be an ordeal. Visiting all the fraternity houses during open rush caused a stir because blacks obviously had never participated in the open rush. It was just expected that they would join the Alphas if they wanted to be part of fraternity life. I remember when I finally did go to the Alpha's rush party, the brothers wanted to know where I had been. When I told them I had gone with my roommates around all the fraternity houses, they were somewhat

Tennis star Paul Gates in action. 1959 *Athena. Courtesy of the Mahn Center.*

surprised and wanted to know all about the experience. It was a little amusing because I did receive two bids from three other fraternities, but they all found out that if they pledged me they would lose their national chapter. Nevertheless, it was a memorable experience.

The spring of 1958 at the MAC Championships at Western Michigan, I lost early in the tennis competition, so I was able to participate in the high jump for track. I placed second in the meet, breaking Ohio University's high jump record in the process. However, what I remember most is the fact that the points I earned helped Ohio U get a surprising second place at the meet. And what was even better was the fabulous steak dinner we had when we stopped to celebrate at a swank restaurant on the way home. Most of us could not eat everything because of the portions we were served, which caused me to have my first experience of a "doggie bag" from a restaurant.

My senior year was quite a year for me. It started off with being elected president of Alpha Phi Alpha fraternity. During Greek Week in the fall of 1959, I was the Alphas' candidate for Mr. Fraternity. All the candidates from each fraternity went through a weekend of interviews with the judges of the event. At the Greek Week Carnival, I was announced as the first runner-up. It was a great accomplishment for me, and I made the Brothers extremely proud.

That same fall at the Varsity O Show, I was tapped by Omicron Delta Kappa, becoming the first black in the history of the school to receive that honor. It caused a great deal of jubilation among my frat brothers as well as many of my friends because most blacks felt that none of us would ever reach that level. I must say that it was a complete surprise to me because I had not planned on attending the show. My best friend from high school, who attended Bowling Green University, had come down for the football game against BG. We had plans to go ice skating. At the last minute, the people in charge of the variety show had to tell him what was happening. He feigned a slight headache and suggested that we attend the show everyone was talking about. When I told him all the tickets had been sold, he revealed two tickets he claimed one of the guys in the dorm had given him because he had to go home on business. I found out later that it was the ODK member who was responsible for seeing that I attended who gave him the tickets.

I remember being upset about having to cut my Christmas break short my senior year (1959) to return to work in the dining hall during an Ecumenical Conference held at OU. In retrospect, I realize what a great opportunity it was because one of the speakers was Dr. Martin Luther King Jr. It was great to say that I had witnessed a speech delivered by him.

During the spring of my senior year, Marion Anderson, the great Met contralto, gave a concert at Ohio University. The night before the concert, I was invited to meet her at a tea given in her honor at President Baker's house. I remember what a charming and gracious lady she was. After the concert, I had the honor of presenting her with a dozen yellow roses from Alpha Phi Alpha.

Another person I had the privilege of knowing was the gentleman who ran the Sundry. I remember his name was Wade, but I don't remember if that was his first or last name. I do know that he was a very congenial man and was genuinely interested in what I planned to do after graduating. We had some very interesting conversations, and I never felt he was being condescending toward me. Our relationship became so trusting that he would let me purchase school supplies and other sundries on credit. He knew that I worked the switchboard in the dorm and was only paid once a month. He was quite willing to wait until I had the money to pay for items I had purchased. I never took advantage of the situation and truly appreciated his kindness toward me.

Dr. Martin Luther King Jr. participated in the 18th Ecumenical Student Conference on the Christian World Mission, held at Ohio University, December 27, 1959, to January 2, 1960. *Courtesy of the Mahn Center.*

My athletic career at Ohio University was unique because I participated in two varsity sports during the same season. I had to arrange my classes so that I could practice high jumping before I went to tennis practice. I don't recall any conflicts between the two. I do know that I would have to get class assignments early whenever we had away matches and meets. There was only one professor who tried to give me a little flack about missing classes for sports, but she had to give in because I had the best average in the class. After my first year of varsity, I did not receive two first-year sweaters but a first-year and a second-year at the same time. My second year of varsity I received another second-year sweater. Overall I had tremendous experiences in the athletic program. I received the Varsity O Senior Award for tennis at the end of my senior year.

All in all, I thoroughly enjoyed my experiences at Ohio University, and I have never regretted my decision to enroll there. For me there will always be fond memories of OU that I will cherish for the rest of my life.

After graduation, I returned to Middletown and began my teaching career at the junior high school I had attended. I spent forty-three years teaching in the public school system in Middletown and Dayton. I basically taught Spanish for most of those years, although I did teach French and English along with Spanish at the beginning of my career. After teaching for ten years, I attended Miami University where I received my master's degree in Spanish. After that, I took a position there with the dean of students' staff as an area coordinator. I supervised the staff and programs in the upperclassmen's dorms. I worked in that position for one year, after which I returned to Dayton and resumed my former position as Spanish teacher at Meadowdale High School. I finished my career there, teaching in a program called the International Baccalaureate, an intensive program where high school students could receive credit by scoring well on the exams.

Throughout my career, my teaching was limited to high schools or foreign languages. I worked as an adjunct professor at Wilberforce University, teaching French, and as an adjunct professor at Sinclair Community College in Dayton, teaching remedial English and tennis. During the summer of 1971 and '72, I was on the U.S. Peace Corps staff in La Pocatière, Quebec, in Canada and in St. Thomas, U.S. Virgin Islands, teaching French to Peace Corps volunteers who were going to French-speaking African countries.

From 1992 to 1995, I taught basic theory of stenography for the Dayton School of Court Reporting. For two years I taught in the Adult Basic Education in Dayton. In 1965 I was selected by the [Ohio] state coordinator of modern foreign languages to be on the state guidelines committee for [setting standards for] teaching Spanish. I was the only high school teacher on the committee. As a Spanish teacher, I chaperoned students to Spain at least fourteen times to have them experience the ultimate in what they were learning in the classroom.

On two occasions my teaching prowess was rewarded. I was presented the Eagle Award for outstanding service to staff development and [service in] the Dayton Public School[s], and in 1998 I received the Educational Alliance's

Excellence in Teaching Award as one of the top ten teachers in Montgomery County. In 1990 I was selected to be in the premier edition of *Who's Who Among American Teachers*. Other outstanding recognitions included being selected in 1972 to be in *Who's Who Among Students in America's Universities and Colleges* and in 1996 receiving a citation for outstanding service to the City of Dayton Police Department.

I continued to play competitive tennis, joining the Dayton Tennis Club, an affiliate of the American Tennis Association. I won several tournaments as a singles player, but my forte was doubles. With different players, I won several ATA Midwestern doubles titles and four ATA national doubles titles. For two years I was vice president of the organization. The two high points of my tennis career were being selected to the Dayton Amateur Tennis Hall of Fame and to my high school's Athletic Hall of Fame for tennis in 1985. My tennis playing ended in 2000 when I developed neuropathy in both feet, but I still enjoy watching the game immensely.

After my second retirement from the school system in 2005, I began earnestly working on developing a program I had envisioned for over twenty-five years: to restore to prominence the poetry of Paul Laurence Dunbar. I have developed a program entitled "Paul Laurence Dunbar Remembered: A Linguistic Approach" in which I discuss the evolution of the Negro dialect and read several of his dialect poems. I eventually want to put the program on a CD and promote it as a supplemental packet to be used in American literature courses in both high schools and universities.

Currently I am content enjoying my retirement. I do a little traveling and am very involved with working in my church.

Continuing Racial Concerns at Ohio University

In 1957, the year that Dorothylou Sands, Alice Jones Rush, Claire Nabors McLendon, and Howard Nolan left Ohio University, and a year after the last of the Soulful Bobcats arrived, prejudice and discrimination were still a concern of Ohio University's administration, of many people in Athens, and of the students who suffered it.

Two letters written in April 1957 offer two points of view. The first, written on April 2 to President Baker from Elsa Sylvester, a representative of the United Church Women of Athens, is somewhat condensed here, and seems to refer more to students from abroad than to Negro students. But her meaning is clear. She asks the question that had been and would be continually asked as Negroes (and whites) debated whether nonviolence or more drastic measures would lead to a more democratic society.

Dear President Baker,

Until we seek your advice, we can have no peace of mind regarding the part the United Church Women of Athens should take in the effort to overcome the Athens race prejudice problem. We know the situation calls for tact and wisdom, and we wonder if the visits of men like Ralph Bunch[e] are possibly *acts of Providence.*

The latest edition of the University *Post* carried a challenge to college men to cooperate in the present campaign for "democracy" in the Barber Shops. (It seems a disgrace such a need exists.)

Does it seem right in a community like Athens, where we are attempting to demonstrate a Christian democracy to guests from abroad, that business men retain *the patronage and good will of our citizens when they are guilty of deeds that undermine and destroy the faith of other nations in American democracy?*

It would be easy to want to institute a crusade! Might that work more havoc than good? Is it better to work *calmly, patiently, and quietly?*

The second letter, written on April 12, 1957, is also to President Baker. This time the plea for a solution to discrimination is from a student.

Dear President Baker,

Why I am taking it upon myself to write to you I do not know, I only know that I must do what I am doing not for my sake but for and on the behalf of my people.

Mr. President, I am a Negro student on your campus, and I am sure that you are quite aware of the Negro situation on and off campus.

I too realize that there is being a fight carried on to put a stop to this discrimination—but let's face it, nothing can really be done without a voice of resentment from the administration and *You*!!

President Baker I ask you, how do *you* and your administration stand on this issue of discrimination?? I look forward to hearing from you very soon, and I only ask that you judge me not by my crude writing or my simple words but by my heart that speaks with truth and sincerity.

Sincerely yours,
Ronald D. Holman

Both letters were answered by Baker and included invitations to come to his office for discussions with him or his staff.

In 1959 and 1961, the state of Ohio enacted its first purposeful civil rights legislation. The 1959 law prohibited discrimination in employment because of race, color, religion, national origin, or ancestry. The statute was amended in 1961 to guarantee all people access to public facilities and private businesses (including restaurants and barbershops) regardless of race, color, etc. The agency of enforcement was the Ohio Civil Rights Commission.

In 1964, Ohio University's catalog contained the school's first nondiscriminatory policy on admission and use of facilities. Applications for housing reflected the policy and no longer required pictures or statements regarding race, religion, or national origin. (Such a policy had been proposed by members of Los Amigos in the 1940s.) The housing application allowed for a roommate preference—of one's own race or another.

However, a 1964 study by the League of Women Voters cites comments by students attending the university in the early '60s that show how much harder it was to change attitudes than laws. One student said, "I went to visit a white friend and his landlord refused to let me go up to his room." Another commented, "there is plenty of prejudice here among the white people, but only shown when we wish to be treated as any other human beings. For instance, like renting a house in any section of town." Another student said he was told at a local motel not to let other guests see him.

Aerial shot of Athens. *Courtesy of Patricia Irwin Kircher, '51.*

One townsperson (a landlady) said she got referrals from hotels saying they were full when she was sure they were not.

The 1950s Soulful Bobcats on Their Own

By the time of the league's study, the Soulful Bobcats, even the graduates of 1960, were beginning to find their paths in the world. Inspired by their loving families, and with the courage and determination to withstand the pressures of college life on a white campus, they had taken the steps necessary to succeed in careers that mattered: the military, business, social work, education, journalism, art, acting, and parenting. As they developed these careers and their families, they became part of the foundation of a new black middle class in an integrated society. They were able, as they and their families had hoped they would be, to give back to those who had supported them and to their adult communities.

Members of the first "Soulful Reunion," held August 9–11, 1991.

"Soulful" Reunion in August

A new summer event is planned for Aug. 9-11— a special reunion for black graduates of the 50s and early 60s. Initiated by two alums from these years, Carl H. Walker '56 of Atlanta and Howard Nolan '57 of Columbus, the "Soulful Reunion" will bring together graduates from a quiet time of change in the life of Ohio University and the nation.

The gathering will be even more meaningful because these grads have been in touch over the years, thanks to the work of Dorothylou Sands, also a chairperson of event, who has maintained a mailing list and newsletter to keep the group spirit lively and memories fresh. Other friends of these alums from the 50s and early 60s are invited to attend as well.

Activities include a welcome kick-off party at the Ohio University Inn, a "walk down memory lane" across the College Green, a reception at Konneker Alumni Center, a banquet with an official University welcome by Provost James Bruning, and, last but not least, dancing to the best loved tunes from the era.

For further information about the program, contact Dorothylou Sands at 213/299-8642, Carl Walker at 404/880-8727, or Patricia Patten Cavender in the Office of Alumni Relations.

The reunion was publicized in the summer 1991 issue of the university alumni newspaper *Ohio Today*.

One group completes some last-minute planning. Seated (*left to right*): Beryl Hannon Dade, Carl Walker, and Patricia Cavender. Standing (*left to right*): Dorothylou Sands, Mitzi Eskridge Johnson, John "Breeze" Smith, Alice Jones Rush, Howard Nolan, and George Reid.

Jo Peters and Gertrude Nolan give support and demonstrate reliability.

Joan Washington Nabors and Beryl Hannon Dade (*foreground, left to right*) register arriving alumni.

Alice Jones Rush and Frances Ramsey Walker greet arriving alumni with a smile.

Several Soulful Bobcats share advice and food. (*Left to right*): Marlene Smith Eskridge, Frances Ramsey Walker, Carl Walker, and Ejaye Johnson Tracey.

Dinner provided the chance for more informal catching up. Seated (*left to right*): Joan Washington Nabors, Rita Osborne, and Jim Thompson (*foreground*).

A group of Bobcats engage in friendly conversation. (*Left to right*): Howard Nolan, Rita Osborne, Beryl Hannon Dade, Mitzi Eskridge Johnson, Ejaye Johnson Tracey, unidentified alumnus, Alice Jones Rush, and Carl Walker.

Sharing smiles and food are (*clockwise*): Alice Jones Rush, Beryl Hannon Dade, Joan Washington Nabors, Rita Osborne, John "Breeze" Smith, Frank Underwood, and Jim Thompson.

Attendees try to remember "who's who" (*clockwise from left*): Frances Ramsey Walker, Monty Robinson, Ejaye Johnson Tracey, and Marlene Smith Eskridge.

One of the pleasures of the reunion was the opportunity to share photographs. (*Left to right*): Leon Ward, Joan Washington Nabors, Claire Nabors McLendon, and Marlene Smith Eskridge.

Grant "Fletch" Latimore and LaQueth Fleming relax at the table, while Bill Henderson and Claire Nabors McLendon converse.

Five Bobcat alumnae smile for the camera. Seated (*left to right*): Etta Bailey Graham and Ejaye Johnson Tracey. Standing (*left to right*): Mitzi Eskridge Johnson, Frances Ramsey Walker, and Alice Jones Rush.

Demonstrating the art of old-style pleasantry (*left to right*): Jim Thompson, Carl Walker, and Bill Henderson.

Among those attending the reunion was this group of photogenic ladies. (*Left to right*): Mitzi Eskridge Johnson, Patricia Patten Cavender, and Ejaye Johnson Tracey.

Carl Walker gains some high-level support in a conference with Richard Polan,
director of Ohio University Alumni Relations.

Grant "Fletch" Latimore and Lois Thompson Green share drinks and
deep conversation.

One group of six pose willingly for a photograph. (*Left to right*):
Monty Robinson, Sylvester Davis, Nyema Baker, Dorothylou Sands,
Kim Haley, and Marlene Smith Eskridge.

Howard Nolan and Claire Nabors McLendon dance, while George Hall watches
(*left, background*).

Ejaye Johnson Tracey and Carl Walker show *their* dance moves.

Ejaye Johnson Tracey and George Hall have a very good time!

EPILOGUE

Passing the Torch

"Let the word go forth from this time and place . . .
that the torch has been passed to a new generation of
Americans—"

President John F. Kennedy
January 20, 1961

THE SOULFUL BOBCATS were an eclectic bunch, as our autobiographical sketches reveal. Despite the differences in backgrounds, it seems that most of us shared the teachings of the older generations of blacks who said, "You cannot change the physical reality of *what* you are—but you can change the mental equation on how you feel about *who* you are." We did not lack pride in who we were, and Ohio University allowed us to maintain that characteristic. Most of us had positive relationships with specific faculty members, many were active in fraternity or sorority affairs, and several actively participated in church activities. Some received athletic scholarships and were recognized for their skills at football, basketball, tennis, or track. At least two of our group were selected for honor societies, one was a finalist in a campus-wide beauty pageant, and at least one other was a *cum laude* graduate. We left the school with friends, skills, and optimism.

Some of us also left with, or soon acquired, marriage partners. Several of the Soulful Bobcats found their spouses from within the group: Marlene Smith and Reginald Haley, Ejaye Johnson and Sherman Robinson, Barbara

Ellis and Les Carney, Shirley Gates and Monte Robinson, Eleanor Christian and Bill Henderson, Etta Bailey and Wilson Gordon Graham, Ella Yates and Leroy Massie, Ada Woodson and Alvin Adams Jr., and Frances Ramsey and Carl Walker. Joan Washington married the brother of Soulful Bobcat Claire Nabors, and there were at least two other marriages between a Soulful Bobcat female and the brother of another Soulful Bobcat male.

We did not, however, or at least most of us did not, leave predicting that we would become the foundation of a newly emerging, black middle class in an integrated society. Prior to the 1960s there were some black professionals—doctors, lawyers, and ministers—but most middle-class blacks were public employees who were almost completely restricted to teaching and nonsupervisory governmental jobs. We hoped to break these old patterns and become highly educated citizens who could command respect in every aspect of American life and penetrate the upper class if we chose to do so.

The 1960s brought about many advances in public and private employment as the 1950s graduates began to integrate the work force in more than token numbers. Inevitably, during the early years of our professional lives we became a generation of "Firsts." Examples of our efforts are shown in the outstanding careers of Howard Nolan, architect and engineer; Cornelius Hopper, MD, and Charles Hefflin, MD, physicians; Sylvester Angel, architect; Rip Nixon, corporate executive; Grant "Fletch" Latimore, DDS, dentist; Frank Underwood, military serviceman and businessman; Alvin Adams Jr., journalist; and Carl Walker, federal government official. Soulful Bobcats who excelled in educational careers include Marlene Smith Eskridge, Beryl Hannon Dade, Joan Washington Nabors, Claire Nabors McLendon, Alice Jones Rush, Dorothylou Sands, Frances Ramsey Walker, George Hall, and Paul Gates. Others achieved high levels of success in the arts: Ejaye Johnson Tracey, singer and actress; Adger Cowans, photographer; and Nelson Stevens, artist. Some of the Soulful Bobcats have been recognized by our alma mater. Four have received either the Ohio University Alumni Association's Medal of Merit or Distinguished Service Award. Two have served on the university's Board of Trustees, two have served on the Ohio University Foundation Board, and one has had a building dedicated in his memory.

Since our graduation, we have lost a number of our group: Alvin Adams Jr., Edwina Banks, Barbara Ellis Carney, Gerald Christian, LaQueth Fleming, Etta Bailey Graham, Bill Henderson, Ted Jackson, Leroy Massie, Milton Morris, Bob Mayo, Howard Nolan, Jean Palmer, Myron Phillips, John "Breeze" Smith, Jim Thompson, Alvin Wesley, Charlie Wilson, Helen Winfield, and Henry Young. As we remember these old friends, we look back and realize that we accomplished much but also left things to be done.

We have been gratified that, in the 1960s, our alma mater emerged as the first of the state's public universities to actively recruit African American students. We are also grateful that, in 1969, Ohio University created the Department of African American Studies, one of the country's first black studies programs, giving its students the opportunity to study their own history and culture. Dr. Patricia A. Ackerman, who earned her BA at Ohio University in 1966, offers further evidence of the institution's efforts to diversify in her 2010 article, "OU Keepsakes from the '60s: Back in the Day, Black Alumni Reunion." Referring to the university's "four firsts from the sixties," she cites the 1963 hire of its first black faculty member, E. Curmie Price; the 1980 appointment of its first African American head coach of any intercollegiate sport, alumnus and '60s cross country and track and field star Elmore Banton; the 1965 recruitment of its first black quarterback, Cleve Bryant, who in 1984 was hired as its first black head football coach; and the 2000 selection of Dr. Ackerman, herself, as the first African American woman to chair the Ohio University Board of Trustees.

Nothing has fulfilled the optimistic outlook of the Soulful Bobcats as much as the 2004 appointment of Ohio University alumnus Dr. Roderick J. McDavis as the school's president. Dr. McDavis is the first African American to hold that position, and he has made increasing diversity a centerpiece of his administration. In his first year, he implemented the Ohio University Faculty/Administrative Staff Diversity Initiative to ensure that more women and minorities were considered for positions. By 2010 the number of full-time African American faculty members had risen to fifty-two and the number of African American administrators to fifty-seven. Though the number of African American undergraduates remains below 5 percent, he has encouraged applications from underrepresented groups with the Urban Scholars Program, established in 2004, and the Appalachian Scholars Program, established in 2005.

We are pleased that Ohio University and its faculty, staff, and students continue to work for a yet more integrated society; therefore, on May 21, 2010, against the above background, twenty-four Soulful Bobcats approved a proclamation:

> The Torch is being passed to a new generation. The flame is powered by a zeal for excellence, a thirst for knowledge, a passion for human-ity, and a commitment to Ohio University. The purpose is to encour-age a completion of the goals, tasks, and responsibilities we undertook and to create new shoulders for others to stand on.
>
> Therefore, we the Soulful Bobcats, students who studied at Ohio University during the decade of the 1950s, are honored to entrust the virtues taught by our parents to the generations of students who have followed us. We wish you success in the challenges we leave you.

May 21, 2010; Athens, Ohio

Ada Woodson Adams	Lois Thompson Green	Shirley Gates Robinson
Sylvester Angel	Grant Latimore	Anne Hunter Rosemond
Harriet Bonner	Clair Nabors McLendon	Alice Jones Rush
Lester N. Carney	Joan Washington Nabors	Dorothylou Sands
Adger Cowans	Lemuel Nixon	Nelson Stevens
Beryl Hannon Dade	Howard Nolan	Carl H. Walker
Marlene Smith Eskridge	EJaye Johnson Tracey	Frances Ramsey Walker
Paul Gates	Evermont Robinson	Frank Underwood

SOURCE NOTES

INFORMATION FOR THE introductory chapter of this book comes from several sources.

For a general outline of the civil rights movement in the 1940s, timelines from several online sites, including history.com and pbs.org, and essays such as James T. Patterson's "The Civil Rights Movement: Major Events and Legacies," from the online site of the Gilder Lehrman Institute of American History (gilderlehrman.org) were helpful.

For background on race relations in Athens, useful sources were *Athens, Ohio: The Village Years* by Robert L. Daniel; *A Significant Presence: A Pictorial Glimpse of the Black Experience in Athens County, Ohio*, by Ada Woodson Adams and Nancy E. Aiken; a 1964 report by the League of Women Voters of Athens titled *The Negro in Athens, A Civil Rights Survey*; and interviews with longtime residents, Carolyn Murphree, who helped write the league's report, and Joanne Prisley, an Ohio University graduate and former acting director and curator of the Athens County Historical Society and Museum.

For information on Ohio University's policies and interactions with African American students, Alden Library's Robert E. and Jean R. Mahn Center for Archives and Special Collections provided rich resources. *Minutes and Resolutions of the President and Trustees of Ohio University, 1922–64*, spelled out the university's official policies on race over time, while the annual yearbooks, the *Athena*, provided more informal, mostly photographic, evidence of African American participation in the life of the school. Documents and letters from the topical files provided information about specific racial incidents at the university between 1920 and 1960, while "Minutes of Los Amigos" were invaluable in describing black students' efforts to improve race relations on campus and in Athens during the late 1940s. Also helpful was *The History and Status of Black Americans at Ohio University* by Connie Perdreau.

AC Clayborne